PUBLIC RECORD OFFICE R[...]

RECORDS OF THE MILITIA
FROM 1757

**Including records of the Volunteers, Rifle Volunteers, Yeomanry, Fencibles,
Territorials and the Home Guard**

BY

GARTH THOMAS

PRO Publications

PRO Publications
Public Record Office
Chancery Lane London
WC2A 1LR

Crown Copyright 1993

ISBN 1 873162 06 5

Printed by MULTIPLEX medway Ltd

PREFACE

In times of national emergency, the Government has recognized the imperative of forming, in addition to the regular armed forces, a military capability dedicated to the defence of the Kingdom. By ancient practice, dating back to Saxon times, all able-bodied men between the ages of 16 and 60 were liable to perform military service within their counties. During periods of national emergency, under the Tudors and Stuarts, statute law had augmented the militia ranks[1]. From 1640, however, the latter were permitted to dwindle for the ensuing century.

This Readers' Guide takes for its point of departure the re-forming of the Militia in 1757, a measure taken by the Government in response to the dangerous military situation arising on the Continent in the form of the Seven Years War. While Britain herself was not directly threatened, the British monarch wore also the Crown of Hanover. Protagonist and antagonist in the Seven Years War were, respectively, Austria and Prussia; and the Kingdom of Hanover allied itself with France, the ally of Austria.

The records left by the various sections of the auxiliary military forces are scattered throughout a number of record classes in the Public Record Office (PRO). Even those records to be found in a single class are rarely arranged in any order that is meaningful to the user. One of the guiding principles that I have adopted has been the need to bring order out of chaos, and so of regrouping references to records of a similar nature or thematic content, and of imposing some discipline upon them, in order to make them meaningful. In that regard, I willingly admit, my regrouping of references may seem at times a little forced, if not arbitrary. Nevertheless, I remain satisfied that readers will now at last be able to find their way around a scattered and very defective collection of records. And with that aim in mind, I have not hesitated to use the same information under differing heads.

This Guide does not deal with the records of Colonial Militia.

The Imperial Yeomanry of the South African War (1899-1902), although containing in its ranks units of the Militia and the Yeomanry Cavalry, was neither Militia nor Yeomanry Cavalry, and its records are discussed in the PRO Records Information Leaflet 59 *British Army records as sources for biography and genealogy.*

Another guiding principle has been the recognition that an indication of the limits of survival of records is as useful to the researcher as knowing where to find the surviving ones. Moreover, although I have not deliberately set out to discover the whereabouts

---

[1] For a discussion of the records of the period that are in the custody of the Public Record Office, see PRO Records Information Leaflet 46 *Militia Muster Rolls, 1522-1640,* and for records deposited elsewhere, J Gibson and A Dell, *Tudor and Stuart Muster Rolls,* Birmingham: Federation of Family History Societies, 1989.

of records that may survive in collections not in the custody of the Public Record Office, where that information has come to my attention, I have included it, but without verification. In addition, and likewise without attempt at verification, I have suggested the reasonableness of seeking a given type of record elsewhere. The user is asked to differentiate between what is stated as fact, and what is suggested as being likely. References to records known to be in the custody of the Public Record Office are followed by a documentary reference number, eg WO 68/139, and with the abbreviation PRO in those instances where I deemed it needful. Most of these records are at the Public Record Office Kew. Where they are at the PRO Chancery Lane this is noted in the text. Documentary references of records in other record offices are suitably identified.

As far as the concept of this guide is concerned, a great debt is owed to the work of Dr P Boyden of the National Army Museum[1]. His approach commends itself by its self-evident, rational simplicity: allowing the creators themselves of the files to tell us exactly what their work comprised and how much of it was set aside in safety for future generations. And it is certainly true that as well as discovering what source material the user has available to him, he needs to know when those sources begin and end and what their limits are.

My thanks also go to Dr A Knightbridge, Mr J Murray, Miss F Prothero and Mr M Stainton, for expert help in the production of this work.

---

[1] P Boyden, *Regimental Records of the British Army, 1859-1900*, in: E T Rice and A Guy (ed), *Army Museum '87*, London: National Army Museum, 1988, pp 36-44.

CONTENTS

1. MILITIA

1.1 Introduction

Creation and evolution of the Militia

As a measure to counter the perceived threat looming on the Continent, the Militia Act 1757 was enacted to re-establish militia regiments in the counties of England and Wales, a policy extended to face the threat arising from the American and French revolutionary wars, the Napoleonic Wars and, later in the nineteenth century, the Crimean War. Recruitment was by means of a sort of conscription, by which the 'Principal' or 'Drawn Men' were drawn by ballot from the lists of adult males (aged 18 to 50, 1758 to 1762; aged 18 to 45, 1762 to 1831) that each parish was required to draw up. The 'drawn man' could delegate his militia obligation to a substitute.

It is important to use the correct terms in identifying the various lists drawn up pursuant to that legislation. The lists of adult males created by each parish are known as Militia Lists (sometimes Militia Ballot Lists); the more limited lists of men chosen from those Militia Lists are known as Militia Muster Lists (WO 13) and Enrolment Lists (WO 68). No Militia List is known to be in the custody of the Public Record Office: such as survive are in the custody of the appropriate county record office, or in the case of Scotland in the record classes Sheriff Court (SC) or County Council (CO) at the Scottish Record Office (SRO). And some Militia records for Scotland may be found in the record class GD in the Scottish Record Office: eg the Seaforth Muniments include lists of men between the ages of 15 and 60 able to bear arms in parishes in Ross-shire in 1798 (SRO reference GD 46/6/45). The value of the two sets of Militia muster records to the military and social historian derives from a comparison made between them; their value for the genealogist and social historian lies in the fact that the lists constitute a national census of the adult male population during the latter half of the eighteenth century. Certain social classes were at first not listed (peers, clergy, teachers, apprentices and 'peace officers'), but a Militia Act of the following year, 1758, allowed of no exclusion. Subsequent Acts extended the amount of information to be included in the Militia Ballot Lists: they are the Militia Act 1802 and the Militia Act 1806. Some Militia Lists have been published through the good services of local history societies[1].

In 1825 discussion began concerning medical practitioners and the Militia ballot, and in 1827 they were granted exemption from it (WO 43/320). By 1827 questions had arisen concerning the legal liabilities of men drawn for militia service pursuant to the Ballot Act, but disqualified from serving (WO 43/298).

---

[1] Eg W G Hoskins, *Exeter Militia List, 1803,* London and Chichester: Phillimore on behalf of Devon and Cornwall Record Society, 1972. See also the information on places of deposit in J Gibson and M Medlycott, *Militia Lists and Musters, 1757-1876,* 2nd edn, Birmingham: Federation of Family History Societies, 1990.

For the regular Militia, a provision of the Militia Act 1757 authorized 'drawn men to arrange for substitutes'. In the case of volunteers, substitutes were not available since the men volunteered and there was no ballot; and so the legislation for the Supplementary Militia Act 1796 could make no provision for substitution (WO 40/9). Among the Militia Sub-Divisional Accounts for the year 1813 are records of fines paid for exemption from Militia service (WO 9/23).

The ballot was generally detested, and revolt against it became a cause of nervousness among members of the higher echelons of the Government. The situation was periodically 'monitored'; and that generated considerable correspondence, which is to be found in the officers' private papers, the majority of which are in the custody of the British Library and amongst other major repositories and private collections. The nervousness was particularly acute in Ireland, and with cause, for it was a combination of Militia and rebels that led to the rising on Easter Sunday 1799 (WO 1/693, f 131).

In Ireland, an additional dimension to the detestation of the Militia service and ballot lay in the local perception of the Militia as a measure of English, protestant domination, particularly as, in 1778, the Militia was constituted to be employed in 'suppressing insurrections and outrageous tumults and in pursuing, apprehending and attending the execution of notorious offenders' (Militia Act, Ireland, 1778). The Irish Militia was disembodied in 1802 (WO 43/400). It was further reduced in strength between 1822 and 1823 through the discharge of supernumerary sergeants, corporals and drummers (WO 43/190). The Solicitor General's report on the Irish Militia Bill, 1 July 1798, is in PC 1/43, bundle A148 (at Chancery Lane).

The records of the apportionment of the Scottish Militia for each county, April 1798, are in PC 1/42, bundle A141 (at Chancery Lane). On 26 November 1798, an Order was drafted for the calling out of the remainder of the Scottish Militia that had been balloted for: the draft, together with the Advocate General's report and the Order published two days later, is in PC 1/43, bundle A148.

Royal warrants of 6 September 1852 and of 8 December 1854 authorized Beating Orders, ie authority to recruit by drumbeat (WO 43/903). WO 32/21A (p 425) contains a memorandum on recruiting of the Militia, dated 1870. The raising of the Militia was a perennial problem: a file of 1807 contains details of the terms of service in the Militia and also the difficulties in raising it (WO 1/612, pp 119, 131, 147, 331), the same year that the Militia was augmented (WO 1/774, pp 67-185, 297, 393). The Selected 'A' Papers and Registers that have been placed in record class WO 41 concern the Militia, Yeomanry and Volunteers, 1810 to 1822. To establish the contents of each year's record, the registers in WO 41/76-98 should be consulted.

Volunteering from the Militia to the regular army was carefully monitored by the military authorities to prevent the transfer of more than the acceptable quota. A record of the regimental quota for enlistment of militiamen into the regular army for the year

1803 is in WO 1/612 (f 189). In 1805 the Home Office issued a circular on the point (WO 40/23); and one of the questions figuring on the Attestation Forms filled in by regular army recruits challenges the latter upon that precise detail. On the other hand, militiamen who had fulfilled their militia service obligations found favourable terms offered them on their transferring to the regular army (WO 40/23). A militiaman normally served three years, later five years, after which he could legally join the regular army. In some cases — particularly non-commissioned officers needed as instructors (WO 3/17), and, following the Militia Act 1796, a soldier or NCO on discharge to pension through Chelsea Hospital (WO 116)—he was authorized to join a local militia unit on full pay (Militia Pay Lists, WO 13). In such cases the taking up of the awarded pension was postponed, an eventuality which was clearly countenanced in the Enrolment Books (WO 68). A militiaman was not attested for service overseas and could not so serve; in order to do so, especially during the period of the American Wars, he could transfer to the regular army; and it is then among regular army records that the research should continue. In 1799 the Irish Militia and Fencibles offered, however, to serve abroad (HO 100/83).

Certain records created pursuant to subsequent Defence of the Realm Acts risk being confused with the Militia Ballot Lists (WO 13). They are the Posse Comitatus Lists of 1798 (Defence of the Realm Act 1797) and the Levée en Masse Lists of 1803-1804 (Defence of the Realm Acts 1803). In effect, those lists constitute additional censuses of the adult male population. But their original purpose was to establish a public list of men not already engaged on military service and who would be available for the purposes of civil defence in case of invasion. Surviving Posse Comitatus Lists are in County Lieutenancy records in the custody of county record offices. Levée en Masse Lists were retained by the compilers, and some subsequently have been deposited in county record offices along with the owner's private papers. Some have been published. Statistical summaries derived from these lists are in County Lieutenancy records and in Privy Council records, the latter being in the custody of the Public Record Office at Chancery Lane.

As part of the general reorganization of the Army undertaken in the 1870s and which culminated in 1881, militia units were attached to the appropriate county regiment as its third (and sometimes fourth) battalion. The new arrangement can be ascertained from the *Army List* of 1882. It is also set out in the introductory note to the listing of record class WO 68 and in **Appendix 3** of this guide.

Politics

The formation of a military force, standing apart from the regular army, could not escape a part in the politics of eighteenth and nineteenth century England, particularly those that opposed parliament to the King. The majority of records that belong to those debates are to be found among the private collections left by the major political figures and military officers of the day, and also in general political comment and parliamentary oratory.

Very few, if any, of those records will be found in the Public Record Office.

Contemporary private papers indicate that the county based structure of the Militia was resented by the regular army. However, it was to prove a strong, sentimental binding force and appears to have underlain the army restructuring policy of Cardwell in the 1870s.

General Records

The Militia Regulations Made by the Secretary at War in pursuance of The Act 15 & 16 Victoria, cap 50; ... (London, 1853; also Sessional papers, House of Commons 1852-1853, 32, lix, 509 [PRO reference ZHC 1/2078]), specified the returns to be made to the Secretary at War by commanders of militia units. They included four specified records of the annual training period, pay lists and monthly returns. Half-monthly returns of recruits and casualties were to be sent by the Adjutant to the Clerk of the General Meeting for the information of the Lord Lieutenant of the county. Of those returns, only the Pay Lists (WO 13/1-3393) and the Monthly Returns (WO 17/974-1002) have survived.

Regimental Books were not mentioned in the *Militia Regulations of 1853*, but seventeen were specified in the *Regulations for the Militia 1894* (HMSO, 1894). They included temporary and permanent regimental order books, records of officers' services, a letter-book, a digest of services and a sub-cash ledger. Each company was, in addition, required to keep four books, though no regulation governing their preservation or destruction was made. The War Office called them in, probably between the two World Wars, then deposited them in the Public Record Office, where they constitute the class of Militia Records (WO 68). However, not all were handed in. Some remain in private hands, others have been placed in regimental museums and county record offices. For example, Somerset Militia books from 1836 have been deposited in the PRO at Kew (WO 68/158-172), but the books prior to 1836 are at the Somerset Record Office, Taunton; Devon Militia books are at the Devon Record Office, Exeter, and the PRO holds only a digest of service of the 2nd (South Devon) Militia in WO 68/139. The conclusion is clear: some units are better documented than others, but all are documented badly.

The Attestations, which the *Militia Regulations of 1853* required to be preserved at regimental headquarters, have been deposited in the PRO, where they constitute record class WO 96. Their arrangement is by regiment, then by alphabetical order of militiaman's surname. They belong, however, in the main to the period 1870 to 1908.

A major source of information about the evolution of the Militia, the Volunteers and the Territorial Army, is constituted by the periodic returns made to Parliament and published in the *House of Commons Sessional Papers*. They should be available in most major research libraries. The PRO holds a set in record class ZHC 1. Included are returns of strengths of units, returns of officers (sometimes even nominal lists) and men, and regulations (covering such matters as organization, pay, training). A complementary set of returns, 1803 to 1815, and indicating the state of readiness achieved on the embodiment of units ordered during the Napoleonic Wars, for both Militia and Volunteers, will be found in HO 50/57-329. Correspondence on various matters concerning the Militia (principally embodiment and regulations) covering the years 1782 to 1840 will be found in HO 50/16-39. In addition, a wide range of matters touching the Militia was considered by the Privy Council. The records are in the Privy Council Registers (record class PC 2 at Chancery Lane). Militia Returns to the War Office, 1806 to 1830, are in WO 24/612-648.

Some County Returns of the Militia were also submitted to the Privy Council and have been placed in record class PC 1, held at Chancery Lane. It is not known why the Privy Council received some Returns but not others. I list those that were included, together with their complete references:

Worcestershire

1789 (PC 1/18, bundle A19)
1790 (PC 1/18, bundle A21)
December 1791 (PC 1/19, bundle A23)
15 January 1794 (PC 1/21, bundle A33)
January and February 1795 (PC 1/24, bundle A43)
January 1799 (PC 1/41, bundle A135)
26 December 1798 (PC 1/37, bundle A148)

Lincolnshire

5 April 1797 (PC 1/37, bundle A115)
7 March 1797 (PC 1/37, bundle A113)
10 March 1797 (PC 1/41, bundle A135)*
2 February 1799 (PC 1/43, bundle A15)
28 March 1809 (PC 1/13/160)

> * A Cavalry Ballot which may have concerned the Militia

Middlesex

1789 (PC 1/18, bundle A19)
1790 (PC 1/18, bundle 21)
January 1792 (PC 1/19, bundle A27)
15 January 1794 (PC 1/21, bundle A33)
January and February 1795 (PC 1/24, bundle A43)

Oxford

February 1798 (PC 1/41, bundle A135)
September 1799 (PC 1/44, bundle A159)

Wigton

May 1798 (PC 1/42, bundle A141)

Cardiganshire

1788 (PC 1/18, bundle A17)

Yorkshire, Durham, Hereford and Northumberland

September 1799 (PC 1/44, bundle A159)

General Militia Returns

August 1796 (PC 1/35, bundle A96)
28 January 1797 (PC 1/37, bundle A112)
1 to 14 February 1797 (PC 1/37, bundle A112)*
3 January 1798 (PC 1/40, bundle A113)
May 1798 (PC 1/42, bundle A141)**

> * Contains both Cavalry and Militia returns
> ** Includes Militia Orders and Schedules

Records concerning the militia responsibilities of the Deputy Lieutenants of the counties, 1816 to 1852, are in HO 51/130, 132-138.

The Royal Warrant for the embodiment of the Supplementary Militia, 1798, is in WO 68/188 (p 1). Indexed records of the arrangements concerning embodiment and disembodiment, 1798 and 1799, are in WO 6/188. Indexed orders as to the embodiment of the Supplementary Militia, 1803, are in WO 1/772, WO 6/190 (p 185), WO 6/191 and WO 6/193 (pp 455-460), and as to the disembodiment of 1802, in WO 6/193 (p 384) and WO 43/31 (p 1). The names of the commanding officers of the English and Scottish units, 1803, are listed in WO 6/176, pp 328-331.

Regimental Movements

Marching orders for the Militia, 1759 to 1820, are in WO 5. The whereabouts of militia units can be determined from the weekly State of the Militia records and Monthly Returns, 1759 to 1925, which are in WO 68. In that same record class are digests of regimental services and regimental histories, together with order books, both general and regimental. It is possible, too, to reconstruct a regiment's movements from information contained in Muster Lists and Pay Books, 1780 to 1878, which are in WO 13.

It should be noted that the date of the embodiment of a regiment is not the date (14 March 1794) given for the appointment of the Colonels (usually holding the rank of Lieutenant Colonel) of the regiments and sometimes of their permanent staff. Embodiment and disembodiment, that is to say the enrolling of men in the regiment and their demobilization, took place when required.

Circulars about camps and the need for uniformity may be found in WO 3/11, 14 and 28. A narrative of the camps may be found in the private papers of Lord Amherst (WO 34/126, 137 and 154). Training seems for the most part to have taken place in the months of February, March and April: for the year 1797 see WO 4/824, papers 50-184. It also seems to have involved a period of 20 days, for which clothing and arms were, pursuant to the Militia Act 1796, ss 25 and 29, supplied (WO 4/828, paper 1). Discussion about punishment for absenteeism from training will be found in a paper of that same year, dated 5 April 1797, in HO 50/28. It was generally considered a good thing that the Militia should train with the regular army (WO 27/40, paper 251). Apparently the camps and training ran smoothly. A month after embodiment 33 units were deemed to be in a reasonable state of readiness (WO 27/40). In 1797 General Dundas could report that most units had been raised and trained (WO 30/65, paper 4). Records concerning the Secretary at War's payments for encampment sites, and concerning refusals of payment, are in WO 4/771. Review Regulations for camps and training are in WO 3/26; in 1779 the Lancashires requested a printed copy (WO 32/157, paper 94).

A sort of 'case study' of the Militia and its activities in 1778 emerges from the War Office correspondence in WO 1/1000.

Tower Hamlets Militia

Because the office of Constable of the Tower of London carried with it command of the Tower Hamlets Militia, records of the regiments are included among the Constable's Office Papers, Official Correspondence and Regulations, 1690 to 1808, in WO 94/67/1. Correspondence about placing the Colours in the Armoury is in WO 94/67/4.

In 1831 the First Regiment of the Tower Hamlets Militia was redesignated the King's Own Light Infantry Militia (WO 43/579).

Records belonging to the years 1853 to 1855, in the 'Old Series' of correspondence of the Secretary at War, concerning the oft presented problems associated with billeting militiamen and horses, tell of an innkeeper who gave money in lieu of lodging to men of Tower Hamlets Militia: the legal opinion in such cases dates to 1846 (WO 43/906).

Channel Islands Militia

Some of the very early records concerning the Channel Islands Militia are to be found among records of the Privy Council. They include the Jersey Militia Laws and Acts of State for Banishment of Persons Refusing to Conform to Militia Laws, referred to Committee on 14 November 1798 (PC 1/43, bundle A148) and the Jersey Militia Act of 7 December 1798 (PC 1/43, bundle A148). A letter dated 5 March 1791, from the Treasury, on the subject of clothing for the Alderney Militia, is in PC 1/19, bundle A23.

A file of the 'Old Series' of the Secretary at War's correspondence, 1840 to 1856, contains records of the Guernsey Militia, a Royal Warrant of 7 September 1843 respecting the enrolment of Chelsea out-pensioners in the Guernsey Militia, together with the printed *Ordonnance de la Cour royale de Guernsey concernant la milice*, 1840 (WO 43/729). In the same series a file, dated 1842-1843, gives details of the establishment and pay of Channel Islands Militia regiments, and includes a detailed report on the Royal Jersey Militia (WO 43/784). Records relating to the redesignation of Channel Islands Militia, 1927 to 1929, are in WO 32/3638 (under code 57A). More general records of the Channel Islands Militia, concerning such matters as service liability and exemptions, overseas service, embodiment, mobilization, and their relations with the Territorials and transfers to them, 1919 to 1948, are to be found in WO 32 (under code 57A). Additional records of proposals concerning the Jersey and Guernsey Militia, in the years 1945 to 1948, are in DEFE 2/1358.

Militia Chaplains

No provision was made in 1760 for the appointment of Militia Chaplains. However, some references concerning Militia Chaplains from 1797 will be found in Home Office entry books to correspondence with the War Office, in HO 50/128.

Militia Quartermasters

Among the 'A and O Papers' of the War Office, paper 968, dated 1884, concerns the 'Old' Militia Quartermasters (WO 33/42). Between 1871 and 1876 the defalcation by a Quartermaster of the Middlesex Militia posed the legal problem whether the adjutant, Captain R McEwen, bore liability for the debt; legal opinion was obtained on the validity of the government bond to cover the debt (WO 43/826).

Complaints against the Militia

Dating to 1761 are bound copies of correspondence between Militia colonels and the Secretary at War, concerning the bad behaviour of the Duke of Richmond's Regiment (WO 43/404). Individuals were named in the complaint of the rope-makers and flax-dressers of Lincoln against a militiaman in 1816 (WO 43/116).

Militia Clerks

In 1852 and 1853 the question of payment of Militia Clerks for general and sub-divisional meetings was raised. It was decided that payment was not applicable for voluntary enlistment (WO 43/901).

Billeting

A disliked burden on the civil population was, understandably, billeting. Records in the 'Old Series' of the Secretary at War's correspondence document the strata-gems employed by innkeepers to avoid it as much as possible. In a file dated 1853-1855 we find that an innkeeper had given money in lieu of lodging to men of Tower Hamlets Militia (WO 43/906). The same file contains a record of increases of daily allowances to householders. Legal opinion of 1843 stated that innkeepers must billet men and horses or provide alternative accommodation for them, and cited the case of Bridge of Alne innkeeper, Alnwick, Northumberland.

Police duties of Militia

Mention has already been made of the police duties of the Irish Militia. In Scotland, on the other hand, it was explicitly stated in 1819 that the Militia was not empowered to assist in the suppression of illicit distillation of spirits and smuggling (WO 43/132). The Suffolk Militia, with a regular army unit, was sent to help the Mayor of Lynn suppress the riots, 27 June 1822, during the Norfolk elections (WO 43/178).

Agent General of Militia

The Militia required agents to handle such matters as procurement of supplies and finances. The records of the office of the Agent General of Militia — records for the period

1803 to 1817 are all that have survived — are in WO 7/110-121. Even so, not all years are represented for all departments. The records of the Public Departments, 1809 to 1811, are in WO 7/110; of the regiments, 1813 to 1817, in WO 7/111-112; of Receivers and Treasurers, 1809 to 1816, in WO 7/113-114; of Clerks of Sub-Divisions, 1809 to 1817, in WO 7/115-118; and of Inspecting Officers, 1803 to 1817, in WO 7/119-121.

1.2   Pay and accounts

The main collection of Militia regimental pay books is in record class WO 13 (years 1780 to 1878). Other pay books will be found in WO 68 (years 1859 to 1925).

In-Letters of the Office of Army Accounts and of the Secretary at War relating to accounts are in the selected 'A' papers in WO 41 (years 1810 to 1822). Amongst other things, they deal with payments to Militia, Yeomanry and Volunteers. That same record class includes registers showing the subject of each paper and its disposal.

Among the records of the Paymaster General's Office are those of the allowances for disembodied Militia, Yeomanry and Volunteers, 1793 to 1927 (PMG 13).

The War Office Accounts in WO 9 include records relating to the Militia. Militia accounts, 1809 to 1818, are in WO 9/13-14. The Journal of Issues of the Militia has not survived in its entirety:

WO 9/15	1760-1761
WO 9/16	1829
WO 9/ 17	1830
WO 9/18	1853-1855

Registers of warrants for the pay of the Militia are in their own idiosyncratic order: WO 9/19 (1795-1803), WO 9/20 (1805-1808), WO 9/21 (1804-1822) and WO 9/22 (1812-1820). The Militia Sub-Divisional Accounts for 1813 (which include records of fines paid in respect of exemption from militia service) are in WO 9/23. The accounts for the South Hampshire Militia, 1780-1782, are in WO 9/24. WO 9/25 contains circulars and similar papers relating to Militia accounts, 1808 to 1814.

Records for the establishment of half pay officers, 1713 to 1824, are in WO 24.

Allowances granted in 1802 to parishes of families of militiamen are discussed in WO 40/ 16. The Law Officers' opinion given in 1804, according to which and pursuant to the Relief of Families of Militiamen Act 1803, wives and families who followed the regiments were entitled to the Parish Relief, is set out in WO 40/20-21. Details of those allowances and payments may be found in parish records, which are not in the custody of the Public Record Office, but in diocesan or county record offices.

Among the general series of registers of papers of the War Office are papers relative to the pay and allowances of other ranks of the Reserve Forces, Militia, Yeomanry and Volunteers: emoluments for the Post-War National Service Militia, 1946 to 1950 (WO 32/11987), and Terms and Conditions of Service for Section 'D' of the Royal Army Reserve (WO 32/13626). Records concerning matters of pay and allowances for officers, 1881 to 1946, are in WO 32 (under codes 39G and 39L). In 1853 and 1854 rates of pay for NCOs and men of the Militia Artillery were raised above those in line regiments, eliciting correspondence between the Home Secretary, Viscount Palmerston, and Secretary at War, Mr Sidney Herbert (WO 43/903).

Regulations concerning pay appear regularly among War Office Circulars and Militia Regulations and Letters in WO 123.

In 1828 the Secretary at War issued a directive to Militia staff, to the effect that local tradesmen must not allow militiamen credit limits beyond their pay limit (WO 43/429).

The Militia units, like the line regiments, were dependent upon the services of the regimental agents and bankers. The records of the Agent General for the Militia, 1809 to 1817, are in WO 7/110-121. The indexes to correspondence of the Militia Agents General, 1803 and 1804, are in WO 2. The failure of the Chichester based bank, Ridge and Newlands, 1841-1842, resulted in payment difficulties for the Duke of Richmond's Sussex Militia and the 2nd Dragoons (WO 43/773).

1.3   Service Records

Officers

Brief details of the service career of a militia officer can be gleaned from information contained in the list of *Officers of the Several Regiments and Corps of Militia*, published by the War Office from 1794 onwards (see **Plate 2**), and in the annually published *Army Lists* which are available on open access shelving in the Reference Room and in the Romilly Room at Kew. Those publications should also be available in major research libraries. The Office of the Lord Lieutenant of Ireland, Dublin Castle, published in 1810 *A List of Officers of ... Militia ... upon the Establishment of Ireland.* A copy of it is available on open access shelving in the Reference Room at Kew. A comprehensive list of such published lists may be consulted on application to the desk in the Reference Room at Kew.

A considerable volume of information concerning the Militia was periodically presented to the House of Commons. Such *Parliamentary Papers* are usually in the form of statistical returns for each unit. Some of them, however, contain names: *Return of the Names of the Colonels and other Officers of the different Regiments of Militia in England and Wales; the Dates of their Commissions; Listing those who have Served in the*

Royal Household Brigade, the Line or the Royal Navy, 1839 (HC 1839, xxxi, 267: PRO reference ZHC 1/1260). A similar return was published the year following, but listing certain regiments only (HC 1840, xxx, 253: PRO reference ZHC 1/1309). It was some years before the next such list was published: *Nominal Return of Officers holding Commissions in Militia and in Volunteer Corps* (HC 1862, xxxii, 583: PRO reference ZHC 1/2816). *The London Calendar, or Court and City Register* (London, 1782-1812) contains, *inter alia*, lists of Militia Officers. Commissions were gazetted in the *London Gazette*, a publication held in major research libraries, and also at the PRO in record class ZJ 1.

Until the middle years of the nineteenth century, the Militia was the responsibility of the Home Office, and early records of militia officers' service are to be found in Home Office archives. In the military correspondence of the Home Office, 1780 to 1840 (HO 50), are lists of commissions into the Militia and the Volunteers, together with returns of service. The Military Entry Books of the Home Office, 1758 to 1855 (HO 51), include records of commissions, appointments and warrants for militia officers, some of which records overlap with the register of commissions in WO 4/9. Sixty-seven original officers' Commissions, mostly on parchment, belonging to the years 1780 to 1874, are in WO 43/1059. Militia commissions were not liable to stamp duty, according to legal opinion of the years 1852 to 1854; but the Secretary at War advised that 'some remuneration' should be made to the Lord Lieutenant's clerks for their preparation (WO 43/883).

Some records of militia officers' service are to be found among the general records of regular army officers' service in WO 76. References to officers appear in various registers of the Militia, 1816 to 1824, in WO 25, and in the Muster Rolls and Pay Lists, 1780 to 1878, in WO 10. Among various private collections of papers presented to the War Office between the World Wars, and thereupon deposited in the Public Record Office in WO 79, are original records of commissions of some Militia regiments, together with lists of officers and other records of officers' service. Commission Books for the Irish Militia, 1794, are in WO 25/118.

References to Militia officers figure, also, among records of the various military establishments, eg half pay, 1713 to 1824, and compassionate list, 1779 to 1812, in WO 24.

In 1780 legal opinions and correspondence on the holding of army rank by militia officers were collected, together with letters of Charles Jenkinson to the Judge Advocate General, Sir Charles Gould (WO 43/403).

Other ranks

Of prime value as sources of information about a militiaman's service career are the Attestation Papers, 1806 to 1915, in WO 96. Attestations are the loose forms that were filled in by the recruit on enlistment and that, in most cases, were annotated throughout his career up to the date of his discharge, so that they constitute effectively a record of his service. Date and place of birth are stated as well. The basic arrangement of records within WO 96 is according to regiment in order of seniority; thereunder, the forms are arranged in alphabetical order of militiaman's surname. The Attestation Papers of Local Militia Regiments, 1769 to 1854, arranged in alphabetical order of militiaman's surname, are in WO 97/1091-1112. Such papers were preserved only in the case of militiamen discharged to pension.

The Pensions Registers of the Royal Hospital Chelsea provide some biographical and service information about militiamen pensioners. The registers of militia pensions, 1821 to 1829 (WO 23), provide the following information: name, age, length of service, cause of discharge and date of death. The information provided in the Admission Books of Chelsea Hospital (WO 116) includes a brief description of the militiaman, his age, place of birth, particulars of service and reason for discharge. Entries in both sets of registers are arranged according to the date of meeting of the Pension Board.

In the absence of such records, biographical information about a militiaman can be sometimes found in the Musters and Pay Books of militia regiments, 1780 to 1878 (WO 13). Moreover, such documents are interesting in their own right, insofar as they provide background information about the regiment's location, expenses and miscellaneous payments. Additional pay lists and other nominal rolls of militiamen will be found among the Militia records, 1759 to 1925, in WO 68.

WO 68 contains also the surviving Enrolment Books which, provided that they were fully filled in at the time, should contain the following information: name, size at enlistment and at 24 years of age, physical description, place of birth (county, city or town, together with parish), place and date of attestation, period of service, former service (and whether entitled to pension from previous military service), promotions, casualties (whether deserted, discharged, transferred or dead) and observations.

The Casualty Books, also in WO 68, the primary function of which was to list desertions, discharges, transfers and deaths of militiamen, often also contain information about marriages and births of children.

The Militia Reserve originated in the 1880s, and provided the regular army with a pool of militiamen who were specially attested for General Service, ie with the Regular Forces overseas in time of war (though subject to certain mitigating conditions). Attestations are in both WO 96 and WO 97.

1.4   Medals

Prior to the South African or Boer War (1899-1902), no medals are known to have been awarded to militiamen as militiamen, and no militia medal roll is in the custody of the Public Record Office.   It follows that a man known to have been a militiaman and to have been awarded a medal will have gained that award in some other branch of the armed forces, the records of which should be searched.   In general, militiamen did not serve overseas, and their service was often for comparatively short periods of time, facts which would in any event reduce the occasions upon which a militiaman might have gained such an award.   Nevertheless, during the opening years of the twentieth century (1901 to 1904), discussion concerning a Militia Long Service Medal and a proposal to institute a new Auxiliary Forces Order generated files now in WO 32/5992, 7245-7247.   Records of the subsequent award of Militia Long Service and Good Conduct Medals are in WO 102/22.

During the South African War a Queen's Mediterranean Medal (1899-1902) was instituted. The medal, for which no bars were awarded, is exactly the same as the Queen's South Africa Medal (QSA) except that the word 'Mediterranean' appears on the reverse and that the words 'South Africa' were deleted.   It was awarded to the third or militia battalions of the following regiments: Royal Northumberland Fusiliers, Royal Fusiliers, West Yorkshire, Loyal North Lancashire, Royal West Kent, King's Own Yorkshire Light Infantry, Seaforth Highlanders and Royal Munster Fusiliers.   The overseas service in respect of which the medal was awarded was for garrison duty in the Mediterranean (Malta), guarding South African prisoners of war.   Records are in WO 100/368, and references are on Attestations in WO 96.

Militia battalions took part in the South African War as regular components of their respective regiments and, consequently, militiamen became eligible for the award of the Queen's South Africa Medal and of the King's South Africa Medal (KSA) with bars. Records are in WO 100.

The Militia Reserve, who were specially attested for General Service with the Regular Army overseas in time of war, were treated as regular soldiers entitled to the QSA and KSA with bars (WO 100).

1.5   Casualties

Lists of casualties among militiamen, 1759 to 1925, figure among militia records in WO 68.   For the period of the South African War, records of casualties of men of the Special Reserve (that is, the militiamen attested for service with the Imperial Yeomanry) may be found among the Casualty Books in WO 129/8-11, and in the Lists of Casualties, October 1899 to August 1902, in WO 108/338 (formerly WO 108/83).

1.6   Deserters

References to deserters may sometimes be found in regimental Muster Lists and Pay Books (WO 13). References to deserters for whose apprehension a bounty was gazetted may be found amongst the subsidiary documents of the Receivers' Accounts of Land and Assessed Taxes (E 182 at Chancery Lane), arranged by county and date. A nominal card index thereto is also available at Chancery Lane. The counties for which such records survive are Bedfordshire, Berkshire, Buckinghamshire, Cambridgeshire, Cheshire and Middlesex. A list of militia deserters, 1811 to 1820, is to be found in WO 25/2934, where in many cases a full personal description is given in addition to details of age, place of birth, date of enlistment, place and date of desertion and how disposed of. Other references to deserters are to be found among the general registers of military deserters in WO 25/2906 and following, and for the years 1744 to 1858 in WO 4/591-654. In July 1799 a proclamation was drafted for the pardoning of deserters from the Militia. A copy together with a report from the Attorney General is in PC 1/44, bundle A156 (at Chancery Lane).

1.7   Courts martial

Surviving records of militia courts martial are in WO 68. Records of militia courts martial may also be found among the papers of the Judge Advocate General's Office in WO 71. The papers and proceedings of the court martial of Captain John Gifford (on the accusation of Major [later Lieutenant Colonel] J Sankey) in 1799 were published in Dublin in 1800, a copy of which is in HO 100/102 (ff 190-238) together with other documents associated with that *cause célèbre*.

Following the riots in Sheffield in 1818, Lieutenant Colonel R Long, South Devon Militia, was prosecuted (WO 43/111).

1.8   Pensions

See also the PRO Records Information Leaflet 123 *Army Pensions Records*.

Militiamen

Records of pensions and allowances for militiamen, 1817 to 1927, and for Volunteers and Yeomanry for some of those years, are in PMG 13/4-50.

There are lists of militiamen eligible for pension up to 1830 among the Subsidiary Documents to the Receivers' Accounts (E 182 at Chancery Lane). The arrangement of those accounts is by county and date. There is no general, nominal index.

Among the Chelsea Hospital pension registers is the Militia Class Book, Christmas 1806 to June 1807 (WO 23/140, ff 1-52). It lists the regiment, the militiaman's name, his age in years, length of service (in years, but sometimes also with indication of months), station (ie rank) in the army, admission date (ie to pension, otherwise date of discharge from the Militia), complaint (ie basis of discharge from the Militia), residence (town and county, not street) and date of muster, either 11, 12 or 26 December 1806. Registers of out-pensioners of Chelsea Hospital, covering militiamen discharged to pension on the ground of disability up to 1913, are in WO 116. The entries are arranged in chronological order of meetings of the Pension Board. In addition, there is a list of pensioners discharged from Militia and Yeomanry regiments, 1821 to 1829, in WO 23/25, where date of death is also indicated; and there are registers of pension payments to disembodied Militia, Yeomanry, Local Militia and Volunteer Corps, 1868 to 1882, in WO 23/89-91. A register of payment of Auxiliary Forces' pensions, 1882 to 1892, is to be found in WO 23/92. Warrants granting pensions to Militia Sergeants are listed in the House of Commons Papers for 1823 (HC 1823, xiii, 63: PRO reference ZHC 1/772).

Among the 'Very Old Series' of the Secretary at War's correspondence are records concerning Militia pensions. For the years 1820 to 1822, there are draft warrants to enable reduced adjutants (NCOs) of local Militia to draw allowances as well as their Chelsea and Kilmainham pensions (WO 43/161). Additional records of this type, 1820 to 1823, and legal advice about them, together with a case, are in WO 43/162. And in WO 43/163 are yet more such records for the year 1820, together with draft affidavits, and records of the half pay establishment, 1817 to 1819. In 1823 the Secretary at War received a Memorial from twelve Militia Regimental Paymasters, who are named, seeking improved retirement terms. The same file contains a letter from Paymaster David Stockford, Oxfordshire Militia, dated 1826 (WO 43/316).

Between 1830 and 1832 an acrimonious exchange of notes took place between the Audit Office and the Secretary at War. The Audit Office required information about half pay and retired pay officers of the British Militia and foreign officers holding civil appoint-ments. The Secretary at War repudiated the claim of the Auditors to question payments sanctioned by him (WO 43/555).

Although not pensioners, it is convenient to mention here that in corporate towns in Scotland, ex-militiamen (named) were, between 1818 and 1824, accorded trading privileges (WO 43/110, 164, 165, 167, 169-171). Two other files of this same 'Very Old Series', both dated 1820, of the Secretary at War's office, dealt with the trading privileges of discharged soldiers and local militiamen in corporate towns, including the case of Stephen Meeks, flesher of Haddington (WO 43/141), and the refusal of 'begging protection' to Charles Spottiswood, pedlar of Peebles (WO 43/142).

Families

Lists of wives and children of militiamen who were eligible for pensions are to be found among the Subsidiary Documents to Receivers' Accounts (E 182 at Chancery Lane). The arrangement is by county and then by date. There is no general, nominal list. Similar lists for Scotland are in the custody of the Scottish Record Office among Lieutenancy and Militia records. A record of payments to wives and children in Midlothian, 1803 to 1815, is in the Exchequer records (SRO reference E. 327/147-158). A file dated 1827-1854 contains persistent claims by militia adjutants for entitlement of their wives to pensions, together with legal opinion (WO 43/450). By 1855-1856 it had been decided that widows of Militia officers were not entitled to pensions: the decision was applied in the case of Surgeon William T Molloy, Northampton Regiment, who died of illness in Gibraltar (WO 43/917).

Between 1829 and 1833 a file was maintained, in the Secretary at War's office, of letters from George Borrow of Willow Lane, Norwich, respecting the disembodied militia allowance made to his brother, Lieutenant John Borrow, West Norfolk Militia, who departed for Mexico leaving two illegitimate children a charge on the parish (WO 43/516).

A nominal list of widows of militia officers in receipt of pension, 1713 to 1829, is in WO 24.

1.9   Families of militiamen

In 1802 an allowance was approved to the parishes of men enrolled in the Militia (WO 40/16 and E 182, the latter at Chancery Lane). In 1804 the Law Officers' opinion held that wives and families who followed the regiment were entitled to the Parish Relief pursuant to the Relief of Families of Militiamen Act 1803 (WO 40/20-21). Details are contained in parish records, which are not in the custody of the Public Record Office but have usually been deposited in the appropriate county record office.

References to next of kin sometimes appear on Attestations (WO 96 and WO 97).

Registers of marriages of militiamen and of the births and baptisms of their children, 1759 to 1925, are in WO 68. Certificates of birth and baptism of children of militia officers, 1793 to 1886, are in WO 32/8903, 8904, 8906-8913, nominal indexes to which are to be found on the open access shelving in the Reference Room at Kew.

2. VOLUNTEERS (1794-1813)

The Volunteers were first raised as an auxiliary military force in 1794. Service was entirely voluntary. Volunteers were not liable to serve outside the Kingdom; but, in time of crisis, provision was made for units to volunteer for service abroad and for individual members to transfer to the Regular Army. In 1799 the Volunteers and other armed associations offered their services for the defence of the country, the record of which is in WO 40/12. Command was vested in the Lord Lieutenant of the county who, in turn, was responsible in this regard, until 1856, to the Home Office. In the military correspondence of the Home Office is to be found correspondence concerning Volunteers, 1797 to 1803 (HO 50/40-56), 1803 to 1853 (HO 51/74-99) and supplementary correspondence, 1794 to 1813 (HO 50/330-356). Other early records, for 1803, are in HO 50/57-312, and a set of the Acts in force relating to the Volunteers, 1799 to 1804, is in HO 51/107. An interesting illustration of local involvement in volunteering is provided by the action of the inhabitants of Hartlepool who, in 1796, formed themselves into Volunteers for the Service of the Coast Batteries (WO 40/8, bundle 22). As a result of the formation, in 1808, of the Local Militia (as distinct from the Militia), based also on limited, voluntary service, the Volunteer Movement dwindled and was dissolved in 1813. The Local Militia was itself dissolved in 1816. The Volunteer Force was revived in 1859.

Surviving records of the Volunteers are mainly to be found in WO 13/4160-4621, but give a far from complete coverage, either in terms of regimental books or in years. A special case is provided by the records of the Royal Preston Volunteers (WO 79/2), which comprise the Minute Books of the Committee of Management, 1797 and 1798; 'Strength Returns' by companies, 1 March 1799; and correspondence for the years 1799 and 1814. They were in private hands until presented to the War Office in March 1939, whence they were deposited in the Public Record Office in WO 79, a record class composed of private collections.

Information about officers appears in the *Army Lists*. Registers of their commissions, 1798 to 1825, are in HO 51/59-73. Their commissions were gazetted in the *London Gazette* (held in major research libraries and by the PRO under reference ZJ 1).

The Establishment Books of the Volunteer Corps, 1802 to 1808, are in HO 51/108-110. Volunteer records for 1804 are in WO 40/21. Increases in the establishment of Yeomanry and Volunteer Corps and the pay and allowances of the newly raised units were documented in 1803 and 1804, and the records together with the Royal Warrant of 22 May 1804 are in WO 43/399. In 1826 the Home Office, at the request of the Secretary at War, submitted a list of the Volunteer Corps of Infantry still existing at 13 May 1826 (WO 43/259).

3. RIFLE VOLUNTEERS (1859-1908)

3.1 General and service records

The institution in 1859 of the Volunteer Force was a further response to contemporary perception of foreign menace. The units were raised pursuant to a provision of the Yeomanry Act 1804, which until 1863 remained the Act under which Volunteers could be raised. They were at first independent and lacking in co-ordination. In 1860 they were brought together into Administrative Battalions, which in 1881 became Volunteer Battalions of line regiments. The financial state and internal organization of the Volunteer Force was the subject of a memorandum in 1870 (WO 32/21A and 21B, p 426). Other records concerning the organization, manning, formation and disbandment of units and also the transfer to the Territorial Force are in WO 32 (under code 14F). The Volunteer Force ceased to exist in 1908, when most of the battalions became part of the Territorial Force.

The monarch's signed appointments to volunteer units, 1914 to 1918, are in WO 103/31.

The Regulations for the Volunteer Force. War Office, 1881 (London, 1881) list various returns that were to be made by Volunteer units, such as returns at inspection by the local District General Officer Commanding, quarterly returns, and regular submission of copies of the Adjutant's diary of instructions given to the corps. Annual returns were to be made on 1 November by the Officer Commanding, together with a nominal roll; and after both documents had been checked at the War Office, the nominal roll was sent to the Clerk of the Lieutenancy 'to be retained for the information of the Lord Lieutenant'. There was no stipulation regarding regimental books as such, apart from the Adjutant's muster book, a record of attendance at drill and diary, which he was to hand on to his successor. In addition to his other duties, the Adjutant had financial responsibility, but no details of his account books are given, except that they were to be handed over to his successor.

The *Regulations* contain no instruction for the permanent preservation of the books and no obligation was placed upon units to keep them. The early independence of the units left decisions on the fate of the books in the hands of the commanding officers. As a result, regimental books are to be found in a variety of places. Some were placed in regimental museums, others were taken home by the officers and incorporated into their private papers, and some were sold or otherwise disposed of and ultimately reached a variety of museums and record repositories. It is clear, however, that the vast bulk of them have been lost. The returns to the War Office have fared little better. The annual returns that were passed to the Clerk of the Lieutenancy should be amongst the Lieutenancy records in county record Offices, but are apparently not. The nominal rolls, the Adjutant's diary and pay lists, held by the War Office, have vanished. All that seems to have survived is an incomplete set of pay lists for Volunteer Staff, 1873 to 1878, in WO 13/4622-4675, and the regimental books of the 10th Battalion, The London Regiment (known as The Paddington Rifles). The unit was raised in 1860 as the 36th Middlesex Rifle Volunteers, was renumbered as the 18th in 1880, became a battalion of the London Regiment in 1908, and was disbanded in 1912. Those records were passed to the War Office and then transferred to the Public Record Office (WO 70/1-21, where they are incorrectly described), and constitute the only set of Volunteer records in official custody. The record of the formation of another regiment, The Victoria Rifles, of the Middlesex Rifle Volunteers, is in WO 43/843.

References to officers appear in the *Army Lists*, where the addresses and other brief details of the local units are given. Among *Parliamentary Papers, 1863*, was published a *Nominal Return of Officers holding Commissions in Militia and in Volunteer Corps* (HC 1863, xxxii, 583: PRO reference ZHC 1/2816). A nominal list, not held by the Public Record Office, was published by H E Harris, *The Alphabetical Volunteer List, Containing the Names of the Officers of the Volunteer Force in Great Britain* (Brighton, 1875).

The Scottish Record Office holds a few records of Volunteer Corps: lists of the Dundee Volunteer Rifle Corps in 1859 (SRO reference MD. 7/1), and a muster roll of the 5th Forfarthshire Volunteer Corps, 1859 to 1886 (SRO reference MD. 7/1).

Despite the loss of Volunteer records, it is usually possible to reconstruct, in outline, the history of many units from the very extensive reports in the contemporary local press. Such newspapers are not held by the Public Record Office, but may be accessible locally or at the Newspaper Section of the British Library at Colindale.

3.2 Medals and Awards

The Volunteer Officers' Decoration was instituted in July 1892, to reward efficient and capable officers of the Volunteer Force, and who had given 20 years' service. Records of its institution, 1892 to 1897, are in WO 32 (under code 50W). The registers, 1892 to 1932, are in WO 330/3-4. The registers of awards of the Volunteers' Long Service Medal made to other ranks, 1906 to 1925, are in WO 102/21.

Other records that include decorations and awards made to Volunteers are mentioned in the discussion of Militia medals (*see* section 1.4).

4. YEOMANRY (1804-1921)

The Yeomanry, like the Rifle Volunteers, were raised under provisions of the Volunteer Act 1804 until 1921, with a modification introduced by the Militia and Yeomanry Act 1901. They were mounted volunteers, their units formed on a county basis and, until the South African War, liable only for home service. Records of the increase in the establishment of the Yeomanry and Volunteer Corps during 1803 and 1804, together with their pay and allowances and the Royal Warrant of 22 May 1804, are to be found in WO 43/399. In 1838, however, the Yeomanry Cavalry underwent a reduction. The records of this, together with a schedule of the regiments, are in WO 43/694. The question of precedence among Yeomanry Cavalry units occupied attention during 1884 and 1885 (WO 32/7238 [under code 6B]). Yeomanry records for the period 1876 to 1942, on a variety of matters, but principally dealing with the transfer of the Yeomanry to the Territorials, are to be found in WO 32 (under code 6B): other matters recorded there concern the state of the Yeomanry, formation of units, terms and conditions of service. The conversion of Yeomanry regiments, 1941 and 1942, is recorded in WO 32/10301(under code 6B).

Between 1833 and 1835 the Irish Yeomanry Corps were reorganized, and the posts of permanent sergeants and drummers were abolished (WO 43/618).

Regulations for the Yeomanry Cavalry, 1832 and 1833, London: War Office, together with the *Abstract of the Regulations, 1821*, London: War Office, are in WO 43/349. *The Yeomanry Regulations: being an abridgement of the Regulations for the Formations and Movements of the Cavalry, adapted to the use of Yeomanry Corps, 1851* (London, 1853) list a number of forms that were to be returned to the Home Office, and after 1855 to the War Office, by the commanding officers. They were chiefly concerned with the payment of the men during the annual training camps and with the supply of arms and equipment. There was no reference to regimental books before the *Regulations for the Yeomanry Cavalry, War Office, 1894* (London, 1894) required each unit to have an Adjutant's diary, musketry register, squadron return books, returns of target practice and equipment's ledger, which were to be produced as required by inspecting officers, and copies to be submitted regularly. The Adjutant was responsible for paying the unit's permanent staff, though there was no mention of pay books.

There was no regulation for the permanent preservation of Yeomanry books. Their preservation is, in general, bad; the best are in regimental custody, others have been noted in drill halls and in private collections. The only returns known to be in the Public Record Office are some Muster Rolls and Pay Lists of 1803 to 1853, in WO 13/3968 -4159.

Yeomanry warrants, 1825 to 1852, are in HO 51/100-102. Letters received by the Home Office from Yeomanry and Volunteers, 1802 and 1803, are in HO 51/103. Registers of Returns for Yeomanry and associated corps, 1794 to 1803, and an index to those returns is in HO 51/104-106. Yeomanry accounts ledgers, 1831 to 1839, are in WO 9/47.

The abolition of the post of Brigade Major in the Irish Yeomanry between 1830 and 1834 led to letters and memorials from redundant officers (named) seeking retirement pay (WO 43/351).

In the English and Scottish Yeomanry Cavalry returns of 1827, certain regiments were named with their complements: Herefordshire, North Somerset, Wiltshire, Royal Linlithgowshire, Renfrewshire, Roxburghshire and Louth (WO 43/223).

Records concerning pensions of adjutants and sergeants of disbanded regiments of Yeomanry Cavalry, 1827 and 1828, are in WO 43/419.

5. THE TERRITORIAL ARMY

5.1 Introduction

Pursuant to the Territorial and Reserve Forces Act 1907, which came into force on 18 March 1908, the Militia was replaced by the Special Reserve. Conditions of service for officers of the Militia joining the Special Reserve, 1907 and 1908, are set out in papers in WO 32/8597-8599 (under code 59A). In 1910 a committee was formed for the organization of the Special Reserve: it reported that year and the following year (WO 32/8603-8605 [under code 14J]). At the same time, the Yeomanry and Volunteers became the Territorial Force (from 1921, the Territorial Army), administered by County Associations. The overall direction of the new auxiliary forces belonged to the Director General of the Territorial Forces, later to the Director General of the Territorial Army. The planning for the Territorials was entrusted to the Territorial Force Advisory Council, of which the following records have survived:

1906-1908*	WO 32/9234-9241	(under code 57A)
1908	WO 32/9696	(under code 6A)
1910	WO 32/9697	(under code 6A)
1914	WO 32/9698	(under code 6A)
1927	WO 32/9699	(under code 6A)
1935-1946	WO 32/9670	(under code 6A)

* Matters concerning provision and planning.

The Council's task included, in addition to establishing matters of general policy for the Territorials and the drawing up of Regulations, such matters as their formation, staffing and manning.

Alongside the regular Territorial Forces, and in accordance with the provisions of s7(6) of the Territorial and Reserve Forces Act 1907, the War Office, between 1908 and 1910, elaborated plans for the creation of a Territorial Force Reserve in three classes: the Territorial Force Reserve, the Technical Reserve and the Veteran Reserve. The *King's Regulations* covering all three branches were issued with Special Army Order, May 1910, presented to both Houses of Parliament, 9 June 1910, and published that same year in London by His Majesty's Stationery Office. The papers are in WO 32/6585. Provisional Orders concerning the Cadet Units were also included.

In 1921 the Special Reserve changed back into the Militia, which in 1924 was replaced by the Supplementary Reserve. The Supplementary Reserve Regulations, 1947 to 1951, are in WO 32 (under code 57B).

Post-war conditions of service for volunteers, both as Territorial Army Officer and other ranks, were examined in files stretching from 1945 to 1948 (WO 32/12868 [under code 59A]).

5.2   General Records

Very few records of the Territorial Forces or Territorial Army have been transferred to the Public Record Office. Those that have been so deposited include the following.

The Territorial Army Precedent Books, 1911 to 1957, are in WO 70/23, 26.

Records of property and finance, 1903 to 1951, are in WO 70/27-30, 32. Other TA records concerning property, taxes and the transfer to the Territorials of lands belonging to the Volunteers and Yeomanry are among the registered papers of the War Office in WO 32 (under code 6D). Returns showing Headquarters of Units and Outlying Drill Stations, 1913, are in WO 114/55. Records of Territorial finances are also to be found in WO 32 (under code 6H).

Records concerning the organization of the Territorials are in WO 32 (see under codes 6 and 14K). Weekly strength returns for home forces are among the Strength Returns of the Army: for September 1914 to November 1920 they are in WO 114/33-51, 56; monthly returns for Territorials' service abroad, November 1914 to December 1917, are in WO 114/52-54. Records concerning titles and distinctions of units are in WO 32 (code 15B), honours and designations of units are in WO 32 (code 16F), and regimental colours and badges in WO 32 (code 43H).

Some Orders of Battle for Territorials have been identified among general army records: WO 32/12775 contains the Mobilization Order of Battle, 1948 to 1950 (2nd revision). The records of the 5th and 6th revisions, 1954 to 1963, and other Mobilization Orders of Battle are believed to be in record class WO 33. They are not specifically identified in the class lists. The Orders of Battle for the Territorial Army Supplementary Reserve, 1950 to 1967, are in WO 32/13821-13826 (under code 6A). Records relating to the anti-aircraft and coastal defence responsibilities of the Territorials are in WO 32 (under code 6C).

The history of the Territorial Force during the First World War, and records concerning its organisation, training and relation with the Volunteers, 1914 to 1918, are in WO 161/ 104 to 112. In 1949 C. 3 Branch, War Office: Department of the Permanent Under Secretary of State, produced a number of historical monographs for the use of students at Staff Colleges; including, in WO 277/6, a study on the wartime contribution of the Territorials: Auxiliary Territorial Service, 1939 to 1945.

WO 70/31 is a file of miscellaneous subjects relative to the Territorials.

The records of the Territorial and Auxiliary Forces Association, 1946 to 1964, are in WO 70/33; Scottish TAFA records are held in the Scottish Record Office in record class MD 7. Other records concerning the membership, tenure of office, regulations, activities and finance of the Territorial Army County Associations are in WO 32 (under code 6D).

Records concerning the regulations, colours and badges of the Officers Training Corps and of the Cadet Corps are in WO 32 (under code 6F). The papers of the Directorate of the Territorial Army and Army Cadet Force, January to May 1946, are in WO 165/105, among the war diaries of War Office Directorates. The status of the Cadets was examined in 1946 and 1947, and the relative papers are in WO 32/11848 (under code 14J). The legal status of the Officers' Training Corps and the Corps' Regulations had been settled in the early years, 1910 and 1911 (WO 32/8675 [under code 14J]). The qualifications and training of officers of the Territorial Army and the Officers' Training Corps had early been a mater of concern, 1907 and 1908, when the draft regulations of the latter were being drawn up and commented upon (WO 32/6566-6569 [under code 59A]).

Among the records of the specialized Territorial units have been preserved those concerning the project for a Territorial Army Medical Corps in 1907 (WO 32 [under code 14F]); the location of medical units of the Territorials in 1908 (WO 32/6558 [under code 6K]); and the redesignation of the Territorial Army Medical Units between 1950 and 1960 (WO 32/13874 [under code 6A]). Those concerning the Royal Monmouthshire Royal Engineers (Militia) are in WO 32/13860 (under code 6A).

As can be clearly seen, the records discussed in this section are very fragmented. Many are presumed to be still held by the regiment (or successor regiment) that created them.

5.3   Service records

The regulations governing the appointment, promotion and retirement of officers of the Territorial Force, 1907 and 1908, are in WO 32/6544 (under code 59A). The basis of selection of officers to command Regular and Territorial Army divisions, 1919, is set out in WO 32/5955 (under code 59E).

No service records of Territorial Army personnel are known to be in the custody of the Public Record Office.   They have been retained by

> CS(R)2b
> Ministry of Defence
> Bourne Avenue
> Hayes
> Middlesex
> UB3 1RF

where staff will, on written application only, and for a fee, make information available to the serviceman himself or to his next of kin.

5.4   Medals and Awards

Records concerning the Territorial Decoration (TD) are in WO 32 (under code 50L). No rolls of the TD are in the custody of the Public Record Office. They have been retained by the Ministry of Defence in the custody of

>   Army Medal Office
>   Government Buildings
>   Worcester Road
>   Droitwich
>   Worcestershire
>   WR9 8AU.

Rules for the award of the Territorial Efficiency Medal and of the Territorial Efficiency Decoration, 1900 to 1903, are in WO 32 (under code 6A). Records concerning the Silver Badge for Long and Meritorious Service, 1933-1934, for the Officers Training Corps and the Cadet Corps, are in WO 32/2726 (under code 6F). Territorial Army records concerning Decorations and Ceremonial are also to be found in WO 32 (under code 6G), among which WO 32/2727 concerns the issue of the Silver Badge, 1935 to 1938. Discussion concerning the eligibility of the 1st Wessex Division of the Territorial Force for the 1914-1915 Star is in WO 32/5331 (under code 50V). For information about army medal entitlements in general, see the PRO Records Information Leaflets 101 *World War One Service Medal Rolls*, 105 *World War One Gallantry Medals Indexes* and 108 *Records of Medals*.

25

6. THE HOME GUARD

In 1940 the Home Guard (originally the Local Defence Volunteers) was formed for home defence; it was dissolved in 1945. The officers' terms of service in the Home Defence battalions were set out in 1941 in WO 32/9979 (under code 59A). Personal records and attestations are in the custody of the Army Medal Office, Droitwich (for address see page 25). Other Home Guard papers may survive in county record offices among the Territorial Army County Associations' records, and others may have been deposited with service records in the Army Medal Office.

In October 1944 several volumes were issued containing the final list of Home Guard officers (WO 199/3210-3217, see **Plate 6**). They were edited along the lines of the *Army Lists*, but each volume presents a separate command[1]. Dates of commission and appointment are given, and indications of regimental and Territorial Army postings.

The Southern Region Home Guard, 1941 to 1945, received considerable attention in railway records: see the publications collected together in British Transport Historical Records, Periodical, Newspapers and Magazines, in record class ZPER 96.

Among the Military Headquarters' Papers, 1939 to 1945, are histories and miscellaneous papers of some Home Guard units:

22 (Tunbridge Wells) Battalion, Kent, May 1940 to April 1944	WO 199/3201
19 Battalion, Kent, May 1940 to December 1945	WO 199/3202
West Sussex Group, August 1945	WO 199/3203
1 (Chichester) Battalion, Sussex, June 1945	WO 199/3204
26 (Worth Forest) Battalion, Sussex, January 1944	WO 199/3205
8 (Burton) Battalion, Staffordshire, 1945	WO 199/3206
1 Scottish Border Battalion, March 1944	WO 199/3207
2 Scottish Border Battalion, December 1942	WO 199/3208
1 Zetland Battalion, January to March 1942	WO 199/3209

Civil Defence came under the jurisdiction of the Ministry of Home Security. In the Registered Files concerning Air Raid Precautions (ARP GEN) created by Home Security (HO 186 and the parallel records in HO 207) are records concerning the Home Guard and other Civil Defence organizations (for both males and females). There is a subject index at the beginning of the record class lists. Another major set of Home Guard records is in HO 199, the Intelligence Branch Registered Files, 1939 to 1950.

---

[1] A similar list is held by the Imperial War Museum.

Under code 66 of WO 32 will be found the general series of registered papers concerning the Home Guard: they are case papers of a generally historical nature, records of legislation, uniforms, pay and allowances. WO 33/1700 concerns Home Guard equipment, 1942 to 1944. Finally, there is a committee report, dated October 1940, in WO 163/414, among the War Office Council and Army Council records. Other related sets of papers are in the Historical Section Files (Archivist and Librarian Series) of the Cabinet Office, which are in record class CAB 106, together with the Ministry of Defence Secretariat Files in CAB 120.

The Operational Papers of the Home Guard are to be found among the records of the Prime Minister's Office, in record class PREM 3[1]. They can be used for identifying the whereabouts of Home Guard units. Home Guard War Diaries are in record class WO 166, War Diaries, Home Forces, 1939 to 1945. Among the war diaries of the War Office Directorates are the reports of the Inspectorate of the Home Guard, June to November 1940, in WO 165/92, followed by the reports of the Directorate of the Home Guard, November 1940 to December 1945, in WO 165/93.

The records concerning the stand-down of the Home Guard in England and similar colonial forces, 1944-1948, are in WO 32/10818 (under code O [A]).

Records of local proceedings have sometimes been preserved in local record offices.

---

[1]See also the study by LB Whittaker, *Stand Down! Orders of Battle for the units of the Home Guard of the United Kingdom, November 1944* (Newport, 1990).

7. FENCIBLE CORPS

The raising of Fencible Corps was yet another means whereby the Government sought to provide for home defence in periods of extreme danger. Unlike the Militia, Fencible Corps were not a continuous service liability. Instead, they were raised only at times when the regular army, or the major part of it, was serving overseas. Service liability was restricted to the Kingdom, but Fencible Corps could volunteer to extend their services abroad. A list of Fencible Corps raised for service in Great Britain and Ireland in 1808 and including those who volunteered for overseas service is in WO 40/25 (bundle 20). Service was voluntary but remunerated: Fencibles received a bounty of 3 guineas and pay and allowances as for the regular army.

Surviving Muster Rolls and Pay Lists for the Fencible Cavalry are in WO 13/3726-3785, for the Fencible Provisional Cavalry in WO 13/3786-3791. They belong to the period 1794 to 1802. The Muster Lists and Pay Books of a mere handful of Fencible regiments, but notably the Isle of Man Fencibles, are in WO 12 (1st Manx Fencibles, 1783 to 1811, in WO 12/10898; 2nd Manx Fencibles, 1796 to 1802, in WO 12/10908; Surrey Fencibles, 1801 to 1802, in WO 12/11093). Records of a disbanding of the 1st Manx Fencibles in 1803 are in WO 40/18, while the records of the Corps of Fencible Infantry for service in the Isle of Man for the same year are in WO 40/19. Other records of Fencible units, including nominal lists, are to be found in the Out-letters of the War Office in WO 4, to which the index is in WO 2/1. A list of Fencible Cavalry units dated 26 May 1796 is contained in a letter on the subject of clothing (WO 4/165, pp 39-40).

The Sea Fencibles were a coastal defence force, recruited from among fishermen and boatmen, under naval command, and to be mobilized in the event of invasion or emergency. The pay lists, 1798 to 1810, are in ADM 28. They consist simply of names of men acknowledging receipt of pay, submitted by officers as vouchers for money expended. They are arranged under district and date.

There is an index to letters from named captains of Irish Sea Fencible and Signal Stations to Army officers, 1808 to 1853, in WO 25/248. It is uncertain where surviving letters are to be found, possibly in War Office In-letters or Admiralty Out-letters (ADM 2). However, a very brief digest of the letters is given in this index.

A Return to the Admiralty, dated 1858, is in ADM 1/5704 (paper 645).

It appears that the majority of records concerning the Fencibles have not survived, although some may still be in collections of private papers or deposited in county record offices.

Surviving records concerning the Fencible Irish Militia, 1799 to 1815, are in WO 1/77-778.

8. BIBLIOGRAPHY

Most units have been the object of an historical study. Users should seek guidance thereto in a major research library. Some general works are listed below.

I F W Becket, *Riflemen Form! A Study of the Rifle Volunteer Movement, 1859-1908*. Aldershot: The Ogilby Trust, 1982.

J Gibson and M Medlycott, *Militia Lists and Musters, 1757-1876*, 2nd edn, Birmingham: Federation of Family History Societies, 1990.

W G Hoskins, *Exeter Militia Lists, 1803*, London and Chichester: Phillimore on behalf of Devon and Cornwall Record Society, 1972.

H McAnally, *The Irish Militia, 1793-1818*, Dublin: Clonmore: Reynolds, and London: Eyre and Spotiswood, 1949.

B Owen, *Welsh Militia and Volunteer Corps, 1757-1908*, Caernarfon: Palace Books. Under that general title has been published to date: vol 1: *Anglesey and Caernarfonshire*, 1989, and vol 2: *The Glamorgan Regiments of Militia*, 1990.

H J Owen, *Merioneth Volunteers and Local Militia during the Napoleonic Wars (1795-1816)*, Dolgelley: Hughes Brothers [1934].

G A Steppler, *Britons, To arms! The story of the British Volunteer Soldier and the Volunteer Tradition in Leicestershire and Rutland*, Worcester: Sutton, 1992.

R Westlake, *The Volunteer Infantry, 1880-1908*, London: Military Historical Society, 1992.

R Westlake and M Chappell, *British Territorial Units, 1914-18* (Men-at-Arms Series, n° 245), London: Osprey, 1991.

R J Weston, *The English Militia in the Eighteenth Century. The Story of a Political Issue, 1660-1802*, London: Routledge and Kegan Paul, and Toronto: University of Toronto Press, 1960.

APPENDIX 1

ORGANIZATIONAL STRUCTURE OF THE MILITIA FROM 1759

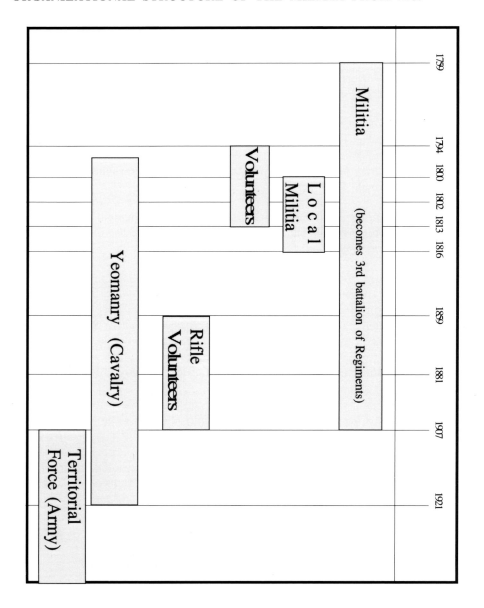

APPENDIX 2

NAMES OF DISTRICTS OF MILITIA IN ENGLAND AND WALES

Anglesey
Bedfordshire
Berkshire
Brecon
Buckinghamshire
Cambridgeshire
Cardiganshire
Carmarthenshire
Caernarfonshire
Cheshire
Cornwall
Cumberland
Denbighshire
Derbyshire
Devon, East
Devon, North
Devon, South
Dorsetshire
Durham
Essex, East
Essex, West
Flintshire
Glamorganshire
Gloucester, North
Gloucester, South
Hants, North
Hants, South
Hants, Isle of Wight
Herefordshire
Hertfordshire
Huntingdonshire
Kent, East
Kent, West
Lancashire, First
Lancashire, Second
Lancashire, Third
Leicestershire
Lincoln, North

Lincoln, South
London
Merionethshire
Middlesex, East
Middlesex, West
Middlesex, Westminster
Monmouth
Montgomeryshire
Norfolk, East
Norfolk, West
Northamptonshire
Northumberland
Nottinghamshire
Oxfordshire
Pembrokeshire
Radnorshire
Rutlandshire
Shropshire
Somerset, First
Somerset, Second
Staffordshire
Suffolk, East
Suffolk, West
Surrey, First
Surrey, Second
Sussex
Tower Hamlets, First
Tower Hamlets, Second
Warwickshire
Westmorland
Wiltshire
Worcestershire
York, East Riding
York, North Riding
York, West Riding, First
York, West Riding, Second
York, West Riding, Third

APPENDIX 3

NAMES OF MILITIA UNITS BEFORE AND AFTER THE CARDWELL REFORMS WITH REFERENCES TO SURVIVING REGIMENTAL BOOKS

One of the effects of the Cardwell Reforms of the regular army was to bring it into line with the county based Militia. It was thence a short distance to amalgamating the two, but not in such a way that their identities were lost. Each County Regiment of the regular army, in theory at least, comprised a battalion for posting anywhere in the Empire, while a second battalion became the depot battalion, which remained at home. The Militia now became a third, and if need be, a fourth, battalion of the County Regiment, and for the most part changed its name.

NAME OF REGIMENT	REFERENCE
Aberdeenshire Militia, Royal *became* 3rd Bn Gordon Highlanders	WO 76/451-452
Amounderness Battalion, Lancashire Militia	WO 79/2
Anglesey Militia, Royal	WO 25/3920
Argyll and Bute Artillery Militia *became* West of Scotland Royal Field (Reserve) Artillery	WO 68/98-117
Argyll and Sutherland Highlanders, 4th Bn *formerly* Royal Renfrew Militia	WO 68/372-374
Armagh Militia *became* 3rd Bn Royal Irish Fusiliers	WO 68/383-401
Armagh Light Infantry *became* 3rd Bn Royal Irish Fusiliers	WO 68/476
Army Service Corps	WO 68/562
Bedfordshire Regiment, 4th Bn *formerly* Hertfordshire Militia	WO 68/375
Berkshire Militia *became* 3rd Bn Berkshire Regiment	WO 68/472

Berwick Artillery Militia *became* part of South East of Scotland Royal Field (Reserve) Artillery	WO 68/78-85
Border Regiment, 3rd Bn *formerly* Royal Cumberland Militia	WO 68/376
Border Regiment, 4th Bn *formerly* Royal Westmorland Militia	WO 68/377
Buckinghamshire Militia, Royal *became* 3rd Bn Oxfordshire Light Infantry	WO 68/242-256
Bute, Argyll and Artillery Militia *became* West of Scotland Royal Field (Reserve) Artillery	WO 68/98-117
Caernarvon and Merioneth Militia, Royal *became* 4th Bn Royal Welch Fusiliers	WO 68/215-217
Cambridge Militia *became* 4th Bn Suffolk Regiment	WO 68/140-157
Cameron Highlanders, 3rd Bn *formerly* Inverness and Highland Light Infantry Militia	WO 68/378
Cardigan Royal Field (Reserve) Artillery *formerly* Cardigan Royal Rifles Militia	WO 68/1-2
Carlow Militia *became* 8th Bn King's Royal Rifle Corps	WO 68/296-305 WO 76/289-290
Carmarthen Royal Field (Reserve) Artillery *formerly* Carmarthen Royal Rifles Militia	WO 68/3-22
Cavan Militia *became* 4th Bn Royal Irish Fusiliers	WO 68/402-405
Cheshire Regiment, 4th Bn *formerly* Cheshire 2nd Royal Militia	WO 68/214
Clare Royal Field (Reserve) Artillery *formerly* Clare Militia	WO 68/23

Connaught Rangers, 3rd Bn *formerly* North and South Mayo Militia *and* Galway Militia	WO 68/319-328 WO 79/1
Connaught Rangers, 5th Bn *formerly* Roscommon Militia	WO 68/475 WO 79/41, 44-45
Cork City Artillery Militia	WO 68/368
Cork City Infantry Militia *became* Royal Munster Fusiliers	WO 68/409
Cork, North, Infantry Militia *became* 9th Bn King's Royal Rifle Corps	WO 68/306-312
Cornwall and Devon Miners Royal Field (Reserve) Artillery *formerly* Cornwall and Devon Miners Artillery Militia	WO 68/24-25
Cumberland Militia, Royal *became* 3rd Bn Border Regiment	WO 68/376
Devon Royal Field (Reserve) Artillery *formerly* Devon Artillery Militia	WO 68/26-27
Devon, Cornwall and Miners Royal Field (Reserve) Artillery *formerly* Devon, Cornwall and Miners Artillery Militia	WO 68/24-25
Devon 2nd or South Militia *became* Devonshire Regiment, 3rd Bn	WO 68/139, 306-312
Donegal Royal Field (Reserve) Artillery *formerly* Donegal Artillery Militia	WO 68/28-30
Donegal Militia *became* 5th Bn Royal Inniskilling Fusiliers	WO 68/221-230
Dublin City Royal Field (Reserve) Artillery *formerly* Dublin City Artillery Militia	WO 68/31-32
Dublin Fusiliers, 4th Bn *formerly* Dublin City Militia	WO 68/491

Dumfries Militia *became* 3rd Bn King's Own Scottish Borderers	WO 68/508
Durham Royal Field (Reserve) Artillery *formerly* Durham Artillery Militia	WO 68/33-34
Edinburgh County Militia *became* 3rd Bn Royal Scots (Lothian) Regiment	WO 68/551-561
Edinburgh Royal Field (Reserve) Artillery *formerly* Edinburgh Artillery Militia	WO 68/35-40
Essex Regiment, 4th Bn *formerly* Essex West Militia	WO 68/257-277, 359-360
Fermanagh Militia *became* 3rd Bn Royal Inniskilling Fusiliers	WO 68/382
Fife Royal Field (Reserve) Artillery *formerly* Fife Militia	WO 68/41
Forfar and Kincardine Royal Field (Reserve) Artillery *formerly* Forfar and Kincardine Militia	WO 68/42-43
Galway Militia *became* 3rd Bn Connaught Rangers	WO 68/328 WO 79/1
Glamorgan Royal (Reserve) Artillery *formerly* Glamorgan Artillery Militia	WO 68/44 WO 69/612
Gloucester Regiment, 4th Bn *formerly* Gloucester Royal North Militia	WO 68/231-241 WO 76/266
Gordon Highlanders, 3rd Bn *formerly* Royal Aberdeenshire Militia	WO 76/451-452
Haddington Artillery Militia *became part of* South East of Scotland Royal Field (Reserve) Artillery	WO 68/78-85
Hampshire Regiment, 3rd Bn *formerly* Hampshire Militia	WO 68/379-381 WO 76/518

Hampshire and Isle of Wight Royal Field (Reserve) Artillery *formerly* Hampshire and Isle of Wight Artillery Militia	WO 68/45-53
Hereford Militia *became* 4th Bn Shropshire Light Infantry	WO 68/278-295
Hertfordshire Militia *became* 4th Bn Bedfordshire Regiment	WO 68/375
Highland Light Infantry, Inverness and, Militia *became* 3rd Bn Cameron Highlanders	WO 68/378
Highland Light Infantry, 3rd Bn *formerly* 1st Royal Lanark Regiment	WO 68/503-506, 522
Highland Light Infantry, 4th Bn	WO 68/489-490
Inniskilling Fusiliers, Royal, 3rd Bn *formerly* Fermanagh Militia	WO 68/382
Inniskilling Fusiliers, Royal, 4th Bn *formerly* Royal Tyrone Infantry Militia	WO 68/71,382
Inniskilling Fusiliers, Royal, 5th Bn *formerly* Donegal Militia	WO 68/221-230
Inniskilling Fusiliers, Royal, 6th Bn *not identified*	WO 68/382
Inverness and Highland Light Infantry Militia *became* 3rd Bn Cameron Highlanders	WO 68/378
Irish Fusiliers, Royal, 3rd Bn *formerly* Armagh Militia	WO 68/383-401
Irish Fusiliers, Royal, 4th Bn *formerly* Cavan Militia	WO 68/402-405
Irish Fusiliers, Royal, 5th Bn *formerly* Monaghan Militia	WO 68/316-318

Irish Regiment, Royal, 3rd Bn *formerly* Wexford Militia	WO 68/173-174
Irish Rifles, Royal, 6th Bn *formerly* Louth Militia	WO 68/313-315
Kent Royal Field (Reserve) Artillery *formerly* Kent Artillery Militia	WO 68/337-340
Kent, Royal West Regiment, 3rd Bn *formerly* Kent West Light Infantry Militia	WO 68/406
Kerry Militia *became* 4th Bn Royal Munster Fusiliers	WO 68/410-412
Kilkenny Militia	WO 68/456-457
Kincardine, Forfar and Royal Field (Reserve) Artillery *formerly* Kincardine and Forfar Artillery Militia	WO 68/42-43
King's County Militia *became* 3rd Bn Leinster Regiment	WO 68/408
King's Own Light Infantry Militia *became* 3rd Bn King's Own Infantry Brigade	WO 68/407, 416-438
King's Own Yorkshire Light Infantry, 3rd Bn *formerly* 1st West Yorkshire Militia	WO 68/448, 474, 499(1)
King's (Liverpool) Regiment, 3rd and 4th Bn *formerly* 2nd Lancashire Regiment	WO 68/488
King's Royal Rifle Corps, 8th Bn *formerly* Carlow Militia	WO 68/296-305 WO 76/289-290
King's Royal Rifle Corps, 9th Bn *formerly* North Cork Infantry Militia	WO 68/306-312
Lanark, 1st Royal Regiment *became* 3rd Bn Highland Light Infantry	WO 68/503-506, 522

Lancashire, 1st, 2nd and 3rd Batteries, Royal Field (Reserve) Artillery *formerly* Lancashire Royal Field Artillery Militia	WO 68/54-58 WO 76/160-162
Lancashire, 2nd Regiment *became* 3rd or 4th Bn King's (Liverpool) Regiment	WO 68/488
Lancashire Fusiliers, 3rd Bn *formerly* 7th Lancashire Rifles	WO 68/500
Lancashire Militia, Amounderness Bn	WO 79/2
Lancaster Regiment, 1st Royal	WO 68/479
Leinster Regiment, 3rd Bn *formerly* King's County Militia	WO 68/408
Limerick Royal Field (Reserve) Artillery *formerly* Limerick City Militia	WO 68/59-63
Lincoln Militia, Royal South *became* 4th Bn Lincolnshire Regiment	WO 68/131-138
Lincoln Militia, Royal North *became* 3rd Bn Lincolnshire Regiment	WO 68/458-462
Linlithgow Artillery Militia *became* part of South East of Scotland Royal Field (Reserve) Artillery	WO 68/78-85
Liverpool Regiment *see* King's (Liverpool) Regiment	
Londonderry Royal Field (Reserve) Artillery *formerly* Londonderry Artillery Militia *formerly* Londonderry Light Infantry Militia	WO 68/64-67
Longford and Westmeath Militia, Royal *became on amalgamation* 6th Bn Rifle Brigade, *prior to amalgamation were respectively* 9th and 6th Bn Rifle Brigade	WO 68/329-336, 439 WO 76/286,292
Louth Militia *became* 6th Bn Royal Irish Rifles	WO 68/313-315

Mayo North Militia and Mayo South Militia *amalgamated and became* 3rd Bn Connaught Rangers	WO 68/319-328
Medway Division, Royal Engineers	WO 68/369
Merioneth Militia, Royal Caernarvon and, *became* 4th Bn Royal Welch Fusiliers	WO 68/215-217
Mid-Ulster Royal Field (Reserve) Artillery *formerly* Tyrone Artillery Militia	WO 68/68-72
Monaghan Militia *became* 5th Bn Royal Irish Fusiliers	WO 68/316-318
Monmouthshire Bn	WO 68/507
Monmouth Militia, Royal	WO 25/3920
Montgomery Militia, Royal *became* 4th Bn South Wales Borderers	WO 68/218-220, 450-455
Munster Fusiliers, Royal *formerly* Cork City Infantry Militia (not identified)	WO 68/409
Munster Fusiliers, Royal, 4th Bn *formerly* Kerry Militia	WO 68/410-412
Norfolk Royal Field (Reserve) Artillery *formerly* Norfolk Artillery Militia	WO 68/341-345
Norfolk Regiment, 4th Bn *formerly* 2nd or East Norfolk Militia	WO 68/123-130, 498
Norfolk Militia, West	WO 68/467-469
Northumberland Royal Field (Reserve) Artillery *formerly* Northumberland Artillery Militia	WO 68/73,121
Oxford Militia *became* 4th Bn Oxfordshire Light Infantry	WO 68/413-414
Oxfordshire Light Infantry, 3rd Bn *formerly* Royal Buckinghamshire Militia	WO 68/242-256

Peeblesshire Artillery Militia *became* part of South East of Scotland Royal Field (Reserve) Artillery	WO 68/78-85
Pembroke Royal Field (Reserve) Artillery *formerly* Pembroke Artillery Militia	WO 68/74-75
Plymouth Division, Royal Engineers	WO 68/370
Portsmouth Division, Royal Engineers	WO 68/371
Queen's Own Light Infantry Militia *became* 5th Bn Rifle Brigade	WO 68/415
Renfrew Militia, Royal *became* 4th Bn Argyll and Sutherland Highlanders	WO 68/372-374
Rifle Brigade, 5th Bn *formerly* Queen's Own Royal Tower Hamlets Militia	WO 68/415
Rifle Brigade, 6th Bn *formerly* Royal Longford and Westmeath Militia	WO 68/329-336
Rifle Brigade, 7th Bn *formerly* King's Own Royal Tower Hamlets Militia	WO 68/407, 416-438
Rifle Brigade, 9th Bn *formerly* Royal Westmeath Militia *became* part of 6th Bn	WO 68/439
Rifle Corps, King's Royal, 8th Bn *formerly* Carlow Militia	WO 68/296-305
Rifle Corps, King's Royal, 9th Bn *formerly* North Cork Infantry Militia	WO 68/306-312
Roscommon Militia *became* 5th Bn Connaught Rangers	WO 68/475
Royal Tyrone Infantry Militia *became* 4th Bn Royal Inniskilling Fusiliers	WO 68/71,382

Scotland, South East of, Royal Field (Reserve) Artillery *formerly* Berwick, Haddington, Linlithgow and Peeblesshire Artillery Militia	WO 68/78-85
Scotland, West of, Royal Field (Reserve) Artillery *formerly* Argyll and Bute Artillery Militia	WO 68/98-117
Scots (Lothian) Regiment, Royal, 3rd Bn *formerly* Edinburgh County Militia	WO 68/551-561
Scottish Borderers, 3rd Bn King's Own *formerly* Dumfries Militia	WO 68/508
Shropshire Light Infantry, 4th Bn *formerly* Hereford Militia	WO 68/278-295
Shropshire Militia (King's) *became* 3rd Bn Shropshire Light Infantry	WO 68/440
Sligo Royal Field (Reserve) Artillery *formerly* Sligo Artillery Militia	WO 68/76-77
Somerset Light Infantry, 3rd and 4th Bn *formerly* 1st and 2nd Somerset Militia	WO 68/441-444
Somerset Light Infantry, 4th Bn only *formerly* 2nd Somerset Militia	WO 68/158-172
Somerset, 1st and 2nd Militia *became* 3rd and 4th Bn Somerset Light Infantry	(see previous 2 references)
South Wales Borderers, 4th Bn *formerly* Royal Montgomery Militia	WO 68/218-220, 450-455
Staffordshire Regiment, South, 3rd and 4th Bn *formerly* Stafford Militia, 1st King's Own	WO 68/523-534
Staffordshire Regiment, North, 3rd and 4th Bn *formerly* Stafford Militia, 2nd and 3rd King's Own	WO 68/470-471
Suffolk Royal Field (Reserve) Artillery *formerly* Suffolk Artillery Militia *formerly* East Suffolk Light Infantry Militia	WO 68/348-358

Suffolk Regiment, 2nd Bn	WO 68/480-482
Suffolk Regiment, 3rd Bn *formerly* Suffolk Militia, West	WO 68/463-466, 492-494, 509-514, 516-521, 549
Suffolk Regiment, 4th Bn *formerly* Cambridge Militia	WO 68/140-157
Surrey Regiment, East, 3rd and 4th Bn *formerly* 1st and 3rd Royal Surrey Militia	WO 68/445 WO 76/64,65,68
Surrey Regiment, West, 3rd Bn *formerly* 2nd Royal Surrey Militia	WO 68/477-478
Sussex Royal Field (Reserve) Artillery *formerly* Royal Sussex Artillery Militia	WO 68/86-87
Tipperary Royal Field (Reserve) Artillery *formerly* 1st or South Artillery Militia	WO 68/88-95
Tower Hamlets, 1st or King's Own Royal Militia *became* 7th Bn Rifle Brigade	WO 68/407, 416-438
Tower Hamlets, 2nd or Queen's Own Royal Militia *became* 5th Bn Rifle Brigade	WO 68/415 WO 76/285
Tyrone Artillery Militia *became* Mid-Ulster Royal Field (Reserve) Artillery	WO 68/68-72
Ulster, Mid-, Royal Field (Reserve) Artillery *formerly* Tyrone Artillery Militia	WO 68/68-72
Wales Borderers, South, 4th Bn *formerly* Royal Montgomery Militia	WO 68/218-220, 450-455
Warwick Regiment, 4th Bn *formerly* 2nd Warwick Militia	WO 68/361-367
Waterford Royal Field (Reserve) Artillery *formerly* Waterford Artillery Militia	WO 68/96-97

Welch Fusiliers, Royal, 4th Bn *formerly* Royal Caernarvon and Merioneth Militia	WO 68/215-217
West Riding Regiment, 3rd Bn *formerly* 6th West Yorkshire Militia	WO 68/215-217
West of Scotland Royal Field (Reserve) Artillery *formerly* Argyll and Bute Artillery Militia	WO 68/98-117
Westmeath Militia, Royal *amalgamated* Westmeath and Royal Longford Militia *became* 9th Bn Rifle Brigade *later became part of* 6th Bn Rifle Brigade	WO 68/329-336, 439 WO 76/286,292
Westmorland Militia, Royal *became* 4th Bn Border Regiment	WO 68/377
Wexford Militia *became* 3rd Bn Royal Irish Regiment	WO 68/173-174
Wicklow Royal Field (Reserve) Artillery *formerly* Wicklow Artillery Militia *formerly* Wicklow Rifle Militia	WO 68/118-120
Wight, Isle of, and Hampshire Royal Field (Reserve) Artillery *formerly* Wight, Isle of, and Hampshire Artillery Militia	WO 68/34-53
Wiltshire Militia, 5th Bn	WO 79/24 WO 76/530
Worcestershire Militia *became* 3rd Bn Worcestershire Regiment	WO 76/493
York, East and North, Artillery Militia *became* Yorkshire Royal Field (Reserve) Artillery	WO 68/121-122
York and Lancaster Regiment, 3rd Bn *formerly* 3rd West Yorkshire Militia	WO 68/447,473, 499
Yorkshire, North, Militia *became* 4th Bn Yorkshire Regiment	WO 68/175-213

Yorkshire, 1st West, Militia *became* 3rd Bn King's Own Yorkshire Light Infantry	WO 68/448, 474,499(1)
Yorkshire, 2nd West, Militia *became* 3rd Bn West Yorkshire Regiment	WO 68/449 WO 76/316
Yorkshire, 3rd West, Militia *became* 3rd Bn York and Lancaster Regiment	WO 68/447,473, 499
Yorkshire, 4th West, Militia *became* 4th Bn West Yorkshire Regiment	WO 76/316
Yorkshire, 5th West, Militia *became* 3rd Bn Yorkshire Regiment	WO 68/535-546
Yorkshire, 6th West, Militia *became* 3rd Bn West Riding Regiment	WO 68/446
Yorkshire Regiment, 3rd Bn *formerly* 5th West York Militia	WO 68/535-546
Yorkshire Light Infantry, King's Own 3rd Bn *formerly* 1st West Yorkshire Militia	WO 68/448,474, 499(1)
Yorkshire Regiment, 4th Bn *formerly* North Yorkshire Militia	WO 68/175-213
Yorkshire, West, Regiment, 3rd Bn *formerly* 2nd West Yorkshire Militia	WO 68/449
Yorkshire Royal Field (Reserve) Artillery *formerly* East and North York Artillery Militia	WO 68/121-122
Yorkshire, South, Regiment *became* King's Own Yorkshire Light Infantry	WO 68/448

APPENDIX 4

SOME ADDRESSES OF RECORD REPOSITORIES OUTSIDE THE PUBLIC RECORD OFFICE

A. Local Authority record offices

Reference has been made in this guide to the fact or possibility that certain records have or may have been placed in county or other local authority record offices. Details of the holdings of each, and information about opening times and addresses, can be found in J Foster and J Sheppard, *British Archives: A Guide to Archive Resources in the United Kingdom,* 2nd edn, London, 1988. In briefer form, similar information is found in *Record Repositories in Great Britain,* 9th edn, HMSO, 1991.

B. Military Museums

B.1 Imperial War Museum

With particular responsibility for material records, written records of a non-official type (private papers, letters, diaries) and captured enemy records, left by the wars of this century, together with a substantial library of printed works, is the

> Imperial War Museum
> Lambeth Road
> London
> SE1 6HZ

where researchers are welcome following preliminary enquiry (071-735 8922).

B.2 National Army Museum

Having wider responsibility and holdings is the

> National Army Museum
> Royal Hospital Road
> London
> SW3 4HT.

The museum mounts displays of material documents left by military engagements that have involved Great Britain. It possesses an important library of printed works together with some copies of public records. It is accessible to researchers following preliminary enquiry (071-730 0717).

B.3 Regimental Museums

Most regiments have established a museum, holding material records and non-public records and in cases some public records. Their addresses are listed in T Wise, *A Guide to Military Museums,* Doncaster: Athena, 1986.

C. Office of Population Censuses and Surveys

C.1 England and Wales

Records of the civil registration of births, marriages and deaths that have occurred in England and Wales since 1 July 1837, are in the custody of the

> General Register Office
> Office of Population Censuses and Surveys
> St Catherines House
> 10 Kingsway
> London
> WC2B 6JP

where researchers in person have access to the lists and order copies of certificates.

Written applications, on the other hand, should be addressed to the

> General Register Office
> Office of Population Censuses and Surveys
> Postal Application Section
> Smedley Hydro
> Trafalgar Road
> Birkdale
> Southport
> Merseyside
> PR8 2HH.

C.2 Scotland

Similar records pertaining particularly to Scotland and Scottish military personnel are held at the

> General Register Office for Scotland
> New Register House
> Edinburgh
> EH1 3YT.

C.3 Republic of Ireland

Similar records pertaining to Ireland and, since 1920, to the Republic of Ireland (Eire), are held at the

General Register Office
Joyce House
8-11 Lombard Street
Dublin 2
Republic of Ireland.

D. Scottish Record Office

Documents described in the text as preserved in the SRO are held at

Scottish Record Office
PO Box 36
HM General Register House
Edinburgh
EH1   3YY.

E. Society of Genealogists

Help in tracing surviving records of militia ancestors may also be obtained from the

Society of Genealogists
14 Charterhouse Buildings
Goswell Road
London
EC1M 7BA
(071-251 8799).

Reference			WO 68

WO 68	Date	Description	
447	1883-1896	3rd Battalion, York and Lancaster Regiment, formerly 3rd West Yorks Militia	Enrolment Book
	1877-1882	Ditto	Ditto
448	1839-1883 1859-1893	3rd Battalion, Yorkshire Light Infantry, King's Own, formerly 1st West Yorks Militia *	Record of Officers' Services (2 books)
449	1803-1813	3rd Battalion, Yorkshire West Regiment, formerly 2nd West Yorks Militia	Enrolment Book
	1815-1821	Ditto	Ditto
450	1792-1854	4th Battalion, South Wales Borderers, formerly Royal Montgomery Militia	Nominal Rolls of officers and men, inspection and clothing returns pay lists, regimental and garrison orders and miscellaneous correspondence
		Ditto	Regulations for exercise of Riflemen, Light Infantry, etc. <u>Printed</u>
451	1845-1908	Ditto	Digest of Services
452	1854-1908	Ditto	Regimental order book
453	1855-1908	Ditto	Mess committee book
454	1873-1908	Ditto	Record of Officers' services
455	1874-1907	Ditto	Inspection reports
456	1855-1860	Kilkenny Militia	Enrolment Book

* Before 1883 the King's Own Yorkshire Light Infantry was called the South Yorkshire Regiment

Plate 1. A detail of a page from the Militia Records class list WO 68, showing the diversity of records and the irregular date ranges typical of the class

John Stuart, Rec.d 25 July

WAR-OFFICE, 10th July, 1796.

LIST

OF THE

OFFICERS

OF THE

SEVERAL REGIMENTS AND CORPS

OF

Fencible Cavalry and Infantry:

OF THE

OFFICERS of the MILITIA;

OF THE

CORPS AND TROOPS

OF

Gentlemen and Yeomanry;

AND OF THE

CORPS AND COMPANIES

OF

Volunteer Infantry.

WITH AN INDEX.

THE FOURTH EDITION.

Plate 2. Title page of the War Office's published Militia List, 1796 (*see p 10*)

MONTHLY RETURN of His Majesty's We...
Colonel Thomas Dyke.

			OFFIC...
		COMMISSION.	

COMPANIES.

		Colonel	Lieutenant-Colonel	Major	Captains
Fra.^k L: Austen's		"	"	"	3
The Honble Lord Visc.^t Marsham's		"	"	"	1
Thos L: Hodges's		"	"	"	1
Isaac Rutton's		"	"	"	1
Thomas Rutton's		"	"	"	1
Fra.^s H: Douce's		"	"	"	1
J: K: Shaw's		"	"	"	1
James Best's		"	"	"	1
J: G: Children's		"	"	"	1
Edward Deering		"	"	"	1
TOTAL		1	"	1	11

ABSENT OFFICERS.

Rank and Names.	Since what time.	By whose Leave.	For what time.
Major Dalton	not joined	being on the	Continent
Captn Shaw	30th May	Colonel Dyke	5th June
N.B. 1 Serjeant on Furlough Sick			
1. Rank and File to Serjeant			
1. D.^o to Drummer			

BRISTOW, PRINTER, CANTERBURY.—1801.

Plate 3. Monthly Return of the West Kent Militia, June 1803, including details of appointments and resignations (WO 17/929, pt 1)

t Kent Regiment of Militia — Commanded by —
Maidstone 1st June 1803.

| | S PRESENT. | | | STAFF. | | | | | Serjeants present | Drummers and Fifers présent | EFFECTIVE RANK AND FILE. | | | | | | | Wanting to Complete. | | | Alterations since last Return. | | | | |
Ensigns	Pay Master	Adjutant	Quarter Master	Surgeon	Mate	Serjeants present	Drummers and Fifers présent	Present and fit for duty	Sick in	Sick in Hospital	On Command	Recruiting	On Furlough	TOTAL	Serjeants	Drummers and Fifers	Rank and File	Joined	Dead	Discharged and not recommended	Discharged and recommended	Deserted
"	"	1	"	1	"	4	2	41	1	"	"	"	0	42	"	"	"	16	"	"	"	1
"	"	"	"	"	"	5	4	37	1	"	"	"	"	38	"	"	"	2	1	1	"	"
1	"	"	"	"	"	3	2	49	2	"	"	"	"	51	"	"	"	6	"	"	"	"
1	"	"	"	"	"	4	1	45	3	"	"	"	"	48	"	"	"	6	"	1	"	3
1	"	"	"	"	"	4	1	49	1	"	"	"	"	50	"	"	"	4	"	"	"	"
1	"	"	"	"	"	4	1	49	3	"	"	"	"	52	"	"	"	6	"	1	"	4
1	"	"	"	"	"	5	2	45	4	"	"	"	"	49	"	"	"	6	"	"	"	"
1	"	"	"	"	"	2	2	48	"	"	"	"	1	49	"	"	"	9	1	"	"	3
1	"	"	"	"	"	3	1	44	9	"	"	"	"	53	"	"	"	5	"	"	"	"
1	"	"	"	"	"	3	2	51	3	"	"	"	"	54	"	"	"	9	"	"	"	"
"	"	1	"	1	"	37	18	458	27	"	"	"	1	406	4	5	354	64	2	3	"	7

Rank and Names of Officers on Duty, and on what Duty.

Vacant Commissions, and by what Means.

Colonel Rich.d James resigned 23d May
L.t E. Chamberlayne resigned 25th May

1. Ens.n to Lieutenant
Ens.n Hooker joined Commiss.n dated 10th May
Ens.n Bishop do. do. dated th.d
W.m Roberts Gent appointed Surgeon

Recruits not joined 232

I do hereby certify that his Majesty's Regulations of 25th May ... respecting settling the ... Accounts have been strictly complied with. —

Tho.s Dyke Colonel

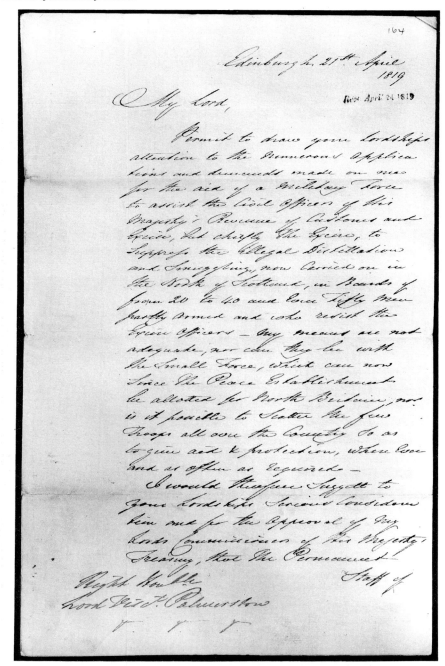

Plate 4. Despatch to Viscount Palmerston concerning Militia policing of illicit distillation and smuggling in Scotland, 1819 (WO 43/132, f 164)

N° of each Description.	Rank and Names.	From	To	At the full Rate of Pay.	At a reduced Rate of Pay as having been in Hospital, or on Board on Transport.	Not entitled to Pay as having been in Prison for Debt, or under conviction for Criminal Offences.	£.	s.	d.	Remarks explanatory of broken Periods of Charge; and of the Periods from and to which the full Rate of Pay is not charged.
	Serjeants.									
1	John Adam	25 June	24 Sept	86	6		7	··	9	On Board Ship 6 days
2	Jas Smith	d°	d°	86	6		7	··	9	d°
3	Dun. Turner	d°	d°	86	6		7	··	9	d°
4										
5										
6										
7										
	Corporals.									
1	Grigor Burgess	25 June	24 Sept	86	6		5	6	3	d°
2	Geo Jamieson	d°	d°	86	6		5	6	3	d°
3	Jas King	d°	d°	86	6		5	6	3	d°
4	Matw Milligan	d°	d°	86	6		5	6	3	d°
5	Geo Ross									
6										
7										
	Drummers (including Drum Major) and Fifers.									
1	Gavin Brown	d°	d°	86	6		5	2	5	Discharged 28 July a Super.num to Glasgow distance. 2/6 Allowed
2	Jas Carruth	d°	d°	86	6		5	2	5	On Board Ship 6 days
3	John Thompson	d°	d°	86	6		5	2	5	d°
4										
5										
	Private Men.									
1	Jas Allan	d°	d°	86	6		4	9	··	d°
2	Wm Baird	d°	d°	86	6		4	9	··	d°
3	Rt Brand	d°	d°	86	6		4	9	··	d°
4	Peter Bell	d°	d°	86	6		4	9	··	d°
5	Andw Black	d°	d°	86	6		4	9	··	d°
6	Peter Burnet	d°	d°	86	6		4	9	··	d°
7	Wm Bart	d°	d°	86	6		4	9	··	d°
8	Geo Calder	d°	d°	86	6		4	9	··	d°
9	Wm Caldwell	d°	d°	86	6		4	9	··	d°

Plate 5. Detail from the Renfrewshire Militia Pay List June - September 1805, Captain Archibald Mair's Company (WO 13/1802)

7

ANTI-AIRCRAFT COMMAND - <u>contd</u>.

NO.1 H.G. A.A. REGIMENT - <u>contd</u>.

71 HAMPSHIRE AND ISLE OF WIGHT H.G.
H.A.A. BATTERY

<u>Major</u>
Pannell, J. P. M., <u>M.B.E.</u>   4/ 1/43

<u>Captains</u>		<u>2nd Lieutenants</u>	
Jackson, W. H.	26/ 1/43	Mitchell, T. W. J.	27/ 5/43
West, F. E.	1/ 2/43	Green, A. A.	27/ 5/43
Legat, T. W.	1/ 2/43	Butchers, J. W.	27/ 5/43
Waltho, A. J.	22/12/43	Skuse, H. G.	27/ 5/43
	1/12/42	Lascelles, C. K. B.	27/ 5/43
Evans, C. V.	21/ 4/44	Wiltshire, D. R.	27/ 5/43
		Dawes, B. J.	24/ 6/43
		Howell, F. H.	24/ 6/43
		Martell, R. H. C.	24/ 6/43
<u>Lieutenants</u>		Royal, A. E.	24/ 6/43
King, F. W.	1/ 5/43	Young, A. V.	15/10/43
Hole, L. W.	24/ 6/43	Hoare, H. R.	22/12/43
Sunderland, J. E.	16/ 5/43		10/ 9/43
Lisby, V. C.	22/12/43	Lockwood, F. H.	22/12/43
Timbrell, G. W.	22/12/43		10/12/43
Dunford, H. A.	17/ 2/44	Bell-Simmonds, M. B.	22/12/43
White, A. L.	7/ 4/44		10/ 9/43
Swanson, J. R.	8/ 4/44	Osborne, J. L.	22/12/43
Beynon, I. R.	19/ 4/44		29/ 7/43
Legg, H. S.	19/ 4/44	Rushton, J. W.	22/12/43
Davis, J. S.	22/ 4/44		29/ 7/43
Harrison, F. N.	3/ 5/44	Apsey, H. J. J.	7/ 4/44
	5/ 4/44	Parsons, M. C.	7/ 4/44
Pearcey, W. C.	9/ 5/44	Collins, B. F.	19/ 5/44
Walton, N. A. C.	13/ 5/44	White, H. L.	9/ 6/44
Dunnings, J.	27/ 5/44	Ward, J. W.	9/ 6/44
Pacey, M. G.	27/ 5/44	Hayward, C. N. H.	9/ 6/44
Luker, H. C.	28/ 5/44	Osgood, W. N.	16/ 6/44
Neish, S. A.	30/ 5/44	Reade, J. B.	6/10/44
Newman, A. J. H.	31/ 5/44		
Child, K.	2/ 6/44		
Sheriton, S. E.	10/ 6/44		
Smith, E. F.	26/ 7/44		
Reeves, C. B.	26/ 7/44		
House, W. C. J.	26/ 7/44		
Smart, S. W.	27/ 7/44		
Bishop, L. N.	15/ 8/44		
Dunning, C. W.	15/ 8/44		
Secker, L. H.	15/ 8/44		
Bell-Simmonds, W. H.	18/ 8/44		
Pooley, A. F.	20/ 8/44		

53826-1(11)

Plate 6. Home Guard, Anti-aircraft Command, Final List of Officers, October 1944, 71st Hampshire and Isle of Wight Battery (WO 199/3210, p 7)

Plate 7. Attestation of George Caldwell, 4th Battalion Highland Light Infantry, 1900. Attestations are the papers the recruit filled in on enlistment, attesting that he would serve in the Militia (WO 96/1099)